THE HALF-MILLION

C.P. STACEY AND BARBARA M. WILSON

The Half-Million

The Canadians in Britain, 1939-1946

UNIVERSITY OF TORONTO PRESS
Toronto   Buffalo   London

ISBN 0-8020-5757-8

Canadian Cataloguing in Publication Data

Stacey, C.P. (Charles Perry), 1906–
The half-million: the Canadians in Britain,
1939–1946

Includes bibliographical references and index.
ISBN 0-8020-5757-8
1. World War, 1939–1945 – Canada. 2. Canada –
Armed Forces – History – World War, 1939–1945.
3. Canadians – Great Britain – History – 20th
century. I. Wilson, Barbara M., 1931–
II. Title.
D768.15.S73 1987   940.53'71   C87-093953-X

This book has been published with the help of a grant from the
Canadian Federation for the Humanities, using funds provided by
the Social Sciences and Humanities Research Council of Canada.

Contents

Preface

ON THE EVENING OF 19 April 1941 a German aircraft dropped a parachute mine on the quiet Surrey village of South Merstham. It killed five inoffensive people waiting at a bus stop, as well as an air-raid warden and a messenger who were just going on duty. It destroyed half of All Saints' Church and demolished the nearby vicarage. The eighty-four-year-old vicar, who was reading in his study, was severely injured. One of his two sisters was killed; the other, like the vicar himself, was in hospital for months.

War conditions being what they were, applications by the congregation to build a 'church hut' where they might worship were at first turned down by the British authorities. The members of the church held services in a hall a mile away. But in due course the war, which had taken the old All Saints' away from them, gave them a new one. Surrey was full of Canadian soldiers. One unit stationed near South Merstham was the 9th Field Ambulance, Royal Canadian Army Medical Corps. In it was serving Corporal George Hedley Wolfendale, a priest of the Church of England who had enlisted in the ranks in 1939. He had made contact with All Saints' and sometimes helped the vicar by taking services. When the catastrophe happened in April 1941 he took over, so far as his military duties allowed, and 'saw that the life and worship of the Church continued,' finding another clergyman to officiate when he could not be there. Late in 1941 Wolfendale was appointed to the Canadian Chaplain Service in the honorary rank of captain. Thereafter he was attached to various units, chiefly of the Royal Canadian Engineers, and through most of 1943 he was with the 1st Canadian Corps Field Park Company RCE. He had not forgotten South Merstham, and now his Engineer connections enabled him to realize the dream of giving the people of the parish a new church.

The chief engineer of the 1st Corps, Brigadier J.L. Melville, approved the project, and in March 1943 the work of building began under the direction of Lieutenant Frederick Eaton of Winnipeg. All the material used (except the cement) was salvaged from the wreckage of the blitzed church and vicarage, and the furniture of the new building, even the cross on the altar, bore the marks of enemy action. In five weeks the job was done, and on 25 April the new temporary church was

The Canadian Red Ensign flies above children attending their first Sunday school
in the church at South Merstham built by the Royal Canadian Engineers. (DHist, DND, 16481-N)

consecrated by the bishop of Southwark, who said, 'I hope that when the church is built again this little building which you have will still house some of the family life of the parish, and all will be told the story of the Easter of 1943, that our Canadian kinsmen went out of their way to build a place in which our people might worship.' The high commissioner for Canada, Vincent Massey, presented a Bible to the new church. The first child christened there was Vivienne Gladys Tanner, the daughter of one of the sappers who built it.

Hedley Wolfendale was present at the consecration of the church. Later in 1943 he went with the 1st Canadian Corps to Italy. He never returned to South Merstham, or to Canada. He was reported missing on 15 May 1944, and is believed to have died of wounds in a German hospital on 11 June. He had been awarded the MBE.

All Saints' parish got a new church in 1952, but as the bishop had hoped the 'little building' put up by the Canadian sappers continued to exist. It serves still as a parish hall, a meeting-place for the Brownies, the Mothers' Union, the Women's Institute, and other parish organizations. It is called Canada Hall in memory of its origins, and has recently been renovated.[1]

The story of Canada Hall is relevant to this book because the building is one of comparatively few material reminders left to recall the fact that hundreds of thousands of Canadian servicemen and women found temporary homes in the United Kingdom for years during the Second World War. It was an extraordinary episode in the social history of the Commonwealth. It is not often that a large slice of the population of one

H/Capt. Rev. Hedley Wolfendale inspired the construction of the new church at South Merstham, Surrey, which Canadian sappers built to replace a church destroyed by a German bomb, 1943. (DHist, DND, 16461-N)

country is picked up bodily, as it were, and set down for years in another country beyond an ocean. The affair is worth remembering and examining, not least because a relationship that had many difficulties in the beginning came in the end to be remarkably warm and successful. That development is the theme of this volume.

This was not the first time a large Canadian military force had come to Britain. In 1914–18 the country was a base and training area for the Canadian Corps that fought in France. Over 400,000 Canadians must have spent some time in Britain during these years, for the record in the Peace Tower in Ottawa informs the visitor that 424,589 members of the Canadian Expeditionary Force left Canada. At the end of 1916, when the force in England was at its peak, there were 131,000 Canadians there.[2] In many ways their experience paralleled that of 1939–46; for instance, many British 'war brides' came to Canada. Nevertheless, the general situation was quite different. The 1st Canadian Division reached England in October 1914 and went to France in February 1915. From that time onward a steadily growing Canadian force was in action with the enemy. New divisions, and reinforcements to fill the depleted ranks of those already in the line, went forward across the Channel; in the opposite direction came shiploads of wounded to recover (if they were lucky) in hospitals in England.

In 1939 Canadians assumed that the experience of the First World War would be repeated: that their divisions would go to France and take their place beside the British Expeditionary Force there. Nobody foresaw the Allied disaster of 1940 on the Continent and the BEF's flight to England. The new 1st Canadian Division, arriving in England in December 1939, was to remain there, on guard against an expected German invasion that never came. Other divisions joined it, until a Canadian army of five divisions was training in the English countryside. Not until July 1943 was a Canadian formation committed to a protracted campaign; not until the summer of 1944 was the whole army to see action. In the meantime they were, perforce, inhabitants of England. Other Canadians were also there: great numbers of airmen, in RCAF squadrons or, more frequently, in those of the Royal Air Force, fighting the Luftwaffe or bombing Germany from British bases. Canadian sailors too, aiding in the defence of Britain, on leave from ships on convoy duty, or preparing to take part in the great combined operations that became practicable as the Grand Alliance grew and found itself able to take the offensive, became part of the British scene and guests of the British people. The story of this Anglo-Canadian experience of 1939–45, now fading into history, is worth recalling and recording.

'Fading into history' is itself an exaggeration. A new generation of Canadians knows little about it. As for the people of the British Isles, it has almost entirely passed from their memory. Even during the war, Canadians sometimes thought that their British hosts were little aware of them. Certainly they were more conscious of the Americans, who were in the end much more numerous and, unlike the Canadians, were not concentrated largely in a few southern counties. Canadians were sometimes heard suggesting that their uniforms were too British; they might have had more recognition if they had worn funny hats, like the Australians and New Zealanders. Books on British life during the war take little notice of the great Canadian community in the country. John Costello's *Love, Sex and War: Changing Values 1939–45* (London 1985), a book mainly concerned with events in the United Kingdom, has one Canadian item in the index – a reference to sex murders. Angus Calder's very long and comprehensive book *The People's War: Britain 1939–45* (London 1971) likewise has one reference to 'Canadian troops' in the index – a passing remark on the Dieppe raid. Following the accepted British custom of lumping all the 'dominions' together, Calder writes, 'The forces from the white Dominions were more like cousins than total strangers' – a comment which so far as the Canadians are concerned needs more than a little qualification. A 'Canadian's' background might be Polish or Italian, or what the English call 'Red Indian'; and in very many cases he was French. Even if, as so frequently was the case, his heredity was purely British, his family might have been in Canada for a century or two, and while he might have a deep sentimental regard for the 'old country,' English society would be utterly strange to him, and adjusting to it was not altogether easy.

How many Canadians went to Britain during the Second World War? Absolutely precise figures are not to be had. The army maintained careful statistics, which show that by VE-Day (8 May 1945) 368,263 men and women of all ranks had arrived in the United Kingdom, and 1767 were then *en route* at sea.[3] This rough total of 370,000 was somewhat increased after the end of hostilities; we shall see in particular that about 1000 members of the Canadian Women's Army Corps went overseas at this time. As for the air force, it is recorded that 93,844 men and women served overseas.[4] Even of those who served in more distant theatres, virtually every one must have spent some time in the United Kingdom; and most of the approximately 94,000 were there for long periods. Concerning the navy, it is reckoned that on 30 April 1945 there were 20,354 all ranks and ratings in the United Kingdom, or serving in ships in European waters or in the convoy escorts that used Londonderry. There must have been considerable numbers of naval men and women who had been in the country but were no longer there in April 1945. The Directorate of History at National Defence Headquarters thinks it likely that some 30,000 naval personnel had been at least briefly in the United Kingdom. This would give us a rough grand total of 494,000 Canadians; in round figures, half a million.

The present book is the result of collaboration between one author who was in England during almost the whole of the war, and another who is a member of the staff of the Public Archives of Canada with special responsibility for military records and who has also pursued the subject in British archives. It attempts to deal with the experience of all three Canadian fighting services. If the army gets more attention than the air force and the navy, it is partly because the army provided the majority of the Canadians in Britain and partly because the army records are more complete. Its war diaries deal with a wide range of events, including many that are social rather than military, whereas the other services tended to keep their records severely official. Some of those records, moreover, have been destroyed. The result is that the sailors' and airmen's relations with the British people are recorded mainly in the few memoirs that servicemen have written, and in the memories of surviving individuals.

The fact that the events of the war days are vague in the minds of the present generation has led us to think it a good idea to provide, by way of introduction, a chapter briefly summarizing the part Canadians óverseas played in the war against Germany. This may serve to place in perspective the happenings in the United Kingdom which are the book's main subject.

We owe debts of gratitude to many individuals and institutions who have helped us in our research. We remember particularly Major J.G. Armstrong, Mrs M.C. Bassett, William Carter, Elizabeth Cleghorn, Daphne Gifford, Lilianne Grantham, Norman Hillmer, David Kealey, Major-General George Kitching, Douglas LePan, Patricia Macoun, Dave McIntosh, Paul Marshall, Bennett McCardle, Marc Milner, Desmond Neill, Murray Peden, Denise Ross, Roger Sarty, Helen Stacey, Brigadier-General Jack L. Summers, Brigadier-General and Mrs W. Denis Whitaker, Mr and Mrs John Woodman, and Glenn Wright. The Master and Fellows of Massey College, Toronto, kindly gave us access to the diaries of the Rt Hon. Vincent Massey. Among the institutions that have been helpful are Public Archives Canada, Ottawa; the Directorate of History, National Defence Headquarters, Ottawa; the Robarts Library, University of Toronto; the Robertson Davies Library, Massey College; and various local record offices in England. We are grateful to Patricia Kennedy for her skilful typing, and to our editor, Rosemary Shipton, for expert assistance in preparing the manuscript for the press.

THE HALF-MILLION

CHAPTER ONE

The Military Task

ON 17 DECEMBER 1939 five great liners moved up the River Clyde towards Greenock. From the shore came welcoming Scottish shouts, answered loudly from the ships. At Greenock a distinguished party waited to greet Major-General A.G.L. McNaughton, commander of the 1st Canadian Infantry Division. These ships carried the 'first flight' of his division, arriving to join the people of Britain in the war against Nazi Germany. This was the advanced guard of a great host.

Canada, after one week of formal neutrality, had declared war on 10 September. The government's war policy was announced on the 19th. So far as the army was concerned, it proposed to organize and train one division as an expeditionary force, to be available if and when required; a second division would be kept under arms as a further measure of preparedness. The units of these two divisions had already been mobilized beginning on 1 September. It soon appeared that the 1st Division would go overseas shortly. A suggestion was made that it might go directly to the south of France, establishing a base area there instead of in England as in the former war; but it was considered that problems of both equipment and morale would make this difficult, and – very luckily, as it turned out – the idea was forgotten.[1]

After landing, the units of the first flight immediately moved off by train southward to Hampshire. They were followed in due course by the balance of the division, which arrived in the Clyde in a still larger convoy at the end of the year. Subsequently, a third flight of transports brought 'ancillary' and miscellaneous troops. By the end of February 1940 there were over 23,000 Canadian soldiers in Britain, most of them concentrated in an area centring on Aldershot, some thirty miles southwest of London.

The 1st Canadian Division on its arrival in England had had only rudimentary training. A certain number of its officers and men, like McNaughton himself, a thirty-one-year-old brigadier-general in 1918, had seen service in the First World War; but in 1939 many of the veterans of that conflict who had sought to enlist were over age or medically unfit. A small number of the men of the division had seen service in the Permanent Force, a rather larger number had had at least

Soldiers of the 1st Canadian Division boarding a
transport at Halifax, December 1939. (DHist, DND, 41720)

some of the elementary training offered by the Non-Permanent Active Militia; but a little more than half were completely raw recruits, and raw recruits they still were when they came to Aldershot.[2] In January 1940, after the men had had their disembarkation leave, a serious program of 'individual training' began, designed to turn them into soldiers. Unit collective training began in March, and divisional exercises were supposed to come in June; but events on the Continent interfered with McNaughton's plans.

A British Expeditionary Force had gone to France at the beginning of hostilities, and, gradually increasing in strength as forces became available, had taken its place on the left of the French Army. Through the winter the front was inactive; this was the period dubbed the 'phony war.' Leisurely planners in London proposed that the 1st Canadian Division should form part of a 4th British Corps, which would join the BEF in the late summer of 1940. Fate decided otherwise. The first unforeseen crisis came in April, with the sudden German invasion of Denmark and Norway. A campaign had to be improvised in Norway, and the War Office asked McNaughton for help: two battalions to take part in a desperate enterprise, an assault on the forts guarding the port of Trondheim. McNaughton agreed (without consulting or informing Ottawa, which his government did not appreciate); what were considered the two best-trained units in the division, Princess Patricia's Canadian Light Infantry and the Edmonton Regiment, were selected and moved to an embarkation port in Scotland. But the Trondheim attack was cancelled (fortunately, it seems today) and the Patricias and the Edmontons came back to Aldershot.

It was the first of many frustrations that year.[3]

The next was not far behind. On 10 May the calm of the Western Front was shattered by a lightning German attack through two neutral states, the Netherlands and Belgium. It was the beginning of a campaign that was disastrous for the Allies. Their forces were cut in two by an enemy thrust to the Channel at Abbeville. By late May the BEF was in desperate danger. In an attempt to ensure its communications with England, small British forces were sent across the Channel to Calais and Boulogne. On 23 May the War Office turned again to McNaughton and his Canadians. The chief of the Imperial General Staff, General Sir Edmund Ironside, told him that he wanted him to go to France and re-establish the road and rail communications through Hazebrouck and Armentières as soon as possible, taking command of the troops in the area, who would be reinforced by a brigade of McNaughton's own division. The 1st Brigade moved to Dover, where it was to embark. McNaughton himself received at Dover on the evening of the 23rd two written directives, bearing the same date and hour, from Major-General A.E. Percival, assistant chief of the Imperial General Staff. It seems clear that the intention was that McNaughton should be free to choose between them, a most unusual expression of confidence in any officer.

The first of these papers followed the lines of Ironside's verbal instructions. McNaughton was to take command of the operation to restore the communications of the BEF. A second brigade of Canadians would be sent to him if it seemed desirable. He was to be prepared 'to run a moving battle with liaison officers and a large proportion of motor cycles' in the absence of normal communications. The other paper directed him to carry out an immediate reconnaissance to Calais and Dunkirk (the British force at Boulogne had already been withdrawn) and report to the War Office whether any useful purpose could be served by landing a force at or near either of these ports. Admiral Sir Bertram Ramsay (then commanding at Dover) later told McNaughton that it was he who suggested to Percival this second paper; he considered that it would be improper to throw a force into the French Channel ports without reconnaissance and consideration. Percival apparently took the responsibility of writing it.

On the night of the 23rd McNaughton crossed the Channel by destroyer with a few staff officers and a small bodyguard. He went first to Calais, still in British hands, and what he saw led him to the initial conclusion that the Canadians should be used to 'strengthen the situation' there. Going on to Dunkirk, he had discussion with French officers there. New information about the battle situation (the road between Calais and Dunkirk was now closed) led him to change his views and to ask permission to return to England for discussion with a War Office representative. A War Office staff officer agreed that this was desirable, and McNaughton and his party re-crossed to Dover. No senior British officer was available for consultation there, and the general drove back to London. There in the late afternoon of the 24th he reported to Ironside in a meeting at which other senior British and Canadian officers were present. All agreed that no purpose would be served by sending a Canadian force to Dunkirk. McNaughton and

A transport carrying men of the 2nd Division draws alongside a floating dock at Liverpool in June 1940. (DHist, DND, 39216)

Ironside went on to a meeting of the British defence ministers and chiefs of staff, presided over by the new prime minister, Winston Churchill, who had taken over on 10 May. There was no final decision, Churchill telling McNaughton that he wished him to consider himself 'at two hours' notice for any eventuality.' But the 1st Canadian Infantry Brigade, which had spent the day on shipboard at Dover, was ordered back to Aldershot: 'A very flat feeling for all of us,' wrote their headquarters' diarist.

The Canadian high commissioner recorded in his diary that just after six o'clock that day 'I met McNaughton in front of the Admiralty waiting for his car, a picturesque figure – steel helmet a little on one side, web equipment and revolver holster – uniform in disarray and with a twenty-four hours' beard.' Massey went with him to Canadian Military Headquarters next door to Canada House and heard his story, and his opinion that 'there is no use attempting to deal with the German thrusts separately for that is what they want – they would like to defeat us piece-meal.'[4] It is worth noting that this time McNaughton had reported to Ottawa what was happening and had been rewarded by a message of encouragement and confidence.

The Dunkirk scheme was not dead. Lord Gort, commanding the British forces in France, was now having to pull them back towards that port with a view to evacuation; and he asked for a Canadian brigade to strengthen the bridgehead position. Early on the 26th McNaughton was told that the previous plan had been revived. The 1st Brigade was again warned for a move, and McNaughton and the senior officer at the Canadian headquarters in London, Major-General H.D.G. Crerar, went to the War Office to discuss the matter. Military opinion there now seemed unanimous that sending more troops into the bridgehead made no sense; but some civilians, notably Anthony Eden, the secretary of state for war, were inclined to differ, and Gort continued to appeal. Only on the afternoon of the 27th was the scheme finally abandoned, and the 1st Brigade, which had been at Aldershot on eight hours' notice with its vehicles loaded, released from tension.

During these discussions more and more soldiers had realized that it was absurd to send additional troops to become involved in a hopeless situation in France when they might be needed at any time for the defence of the United Kingdom. The Canadians now became part of this defence. On 26 May McNaughton had suggested that his division should be organized in mobile groups and moved to a central area whence it could counter-attack an enemy landing anywhere in southern England. On the 29th the 1st Division and the Canadian ancillary troops, organized in a self-contained body known as Canadian Force, began to move to the Northampton area, considered suitable for this purpose. The Canadians got a great reception from the people of Northampton and the neighbouring communities; but their stay there was short. Events in France again seemed to call for their presence in the theatre of operations.

The Dunkirk evacuation was completed on 4 June. The bulk of Gort's army had been successfully brought back to England; but it was without its heavy equipment and for the moment virtually disarmed. However, a large French force, and a few British formations, were still in the field south of the Somme.

Soldiers of the 48th Highlanders of Canada break for lunch
in a gorse-laden field at Aldershot, March 1940. (DHist, DND, 5 23)

Men of the 1st Canadian Division leave Aldershot en route,
it was believed, for the Norwegian campaign. Their expedition was cancelled. (DHist, DND, 41721)

The British government thought it essential, if the French were to be kept in the war, to reconstitute the BEF in France; but very few troops were available for the purpose – actually, only two divisions, the 52nd and the 1st Canadian. The 52nd began to move at once; the Canadians, released from their home-defence task when the Germans launched a new offensive in France on 5 June, were to follow. McNaughton's understanding, after conference with Lieutenant-General Sir Alan Brooke, who was to command the Second BEF, was that his division would land at Brest, assemble northeast of that port, and be prepared to join the other components of Brooke's force in the vicinity of Rennes, the idea being to hold the Breton peninsula as a sort of 'redoubt' – not really a hopeful scheme in the circumstances.

Unfortunately, the British 'Movement Control' authorities at Brest had received orders of a different sort, and when the Canadians began landing there they were pushed off up the country by bits and pieces. Some went by rail, some by road. The 1st Infantry Brigade and the 1st Field Regiment, Royal Canadian Horse Artillery, were in the lead, and were in fact the only Canadians to get to France. They landed on 12 and 13 June. By the 14th they were scattered across northwestern France, the most advanced troops being at Sablé-sur-Sarthe, northeast of Angers. McNaughton was at Plymouth with his advanced headquarters, waiting to embark and ignorant of what was happening on the far side of the Channel. On this day General Brooke, after discussions with the French command which showed that the French army was in a state of disintegration, recommended evacuation, and London agreed. The Canadian movement was put into reverse.

By great good fortune, virtually all the Canadians in France got safely back to England. The 48th Highlanders of Canada reached the coast not at Brest but at St Malo, but as luck would have it there was a British transport there which had room for them. Only one Canadian soldier became a prisoner of war. Once again, the Canadians came back to Aldershot without meeting the enemy.

McNaughton was disgusted at the mishandling of his division, making perhaps too little allowance for the conditions of the moment; and he was inclined to blame Brooke. But there were more important things to think of. To his old friend General Sir John Dill, who had now become chief of the Imperial General Staff, he wrote on 29 June:

We are now squarely set for what I have long thought was the important task, the defence of these islands. Two out of three of our Brigade Groups [the 1st Brigade's transport had been lost in France] and our reserve of Artillery, Engineers, Machine Gun Battalions, etc., all on wheels, are poised to go in any direction and you and the C.-in-C. [Home Forces] can count on a quick moving, hard hitting, determined force which will be prompt to execute your orders.

There are many lessons to be learned from our experience and sometime I hope we can go over them together but, meanwhile, we have other work to do and you can be sure that we stand with you with all our hearts.

The situation, indeed, was thoroughly desperate. France, the great power whose army had been the alliance's chief

The signal section of the Seaforth Highlanders of Canada swing along a Kentish lane in 1940, with a traffic jam forming behind them.
(DHist, DND, 17)

resource on land, was suddenly out of the war, and the French defeat had encouraged Italy to take the plunge and join Germany. Against these antagonists the Commonwealth now stood alone. Britain confronted the possibility of invasion, and for the moment the losses of equipment in France had left the British army incapable of effective fighting. The 52nd Division had got back from France, but without a great part of its transport. The most advanced British divisions were the 3rd (Major-General B.L. Montgomery), which however had been only 4500 strong after its return from Dunkirk, and the 43rd, which was 'rather backward' in training and equipment. It was fortunate that only one Canadian brigade had got to France; the rest of the 1st Division still had its transport. It was one of the very few formations that could be considered even remotely fit for a task of mobile counter-attack. Accordingly, Canadian Force was reconstituted, and on 23 June it began to move to the vicinity of Oxford, a suitable position for a mobile reserve. On the 25th McNaughton reviewed the situation in a conference at his headquarters outside Oxford: 'The G.O.C. stated that we are a mobile reserve with a 360 degree front; and may have to operate anywhere in Great Britain from the South coast, to Scotland, or in Wales. We carry, together with the 4 Corps under Lieutenant-General [F.P.] Nosworthy a serious responsibility. The Cdn Force and two Tk Bns of the 4 Corps with some Lt Armd Units comprise the only mobile force immediately available in Great Britain. These will be reinforced shortly by the 43 Div.'

As reorganization proceeded and new equipment began to come to hand, plans were changed. On 26 June McNaughton

A scene familiar in southern England in the years 1940–4:
Canadians returning from field training. (PAC / DND, PA 137184)

was told that it was now proposed to have two corps in mobile reserve, one under Nosworthy north of the Thames, and one under McNaughton himself south of the river. This latter would consist of the 1st Canadian Division, the 1st Armoured Division, reconstituted after having lost heavily in France, and the 'New Zealand Force' of two infantry brigades and some artillery, which had lately arrived in England. The Canadian government agreed to this new appointment for McNaughton, who was promoted to lieutenant-general. The new '7th Corps' came into existence on 21 July, with its headquarters at Headley Court, near Leatherhead, Surrey. The Canadian brigade groups moved to Surrey in the course of July, and became acquainted with a pleasant county with which the Canadians were to be particularly associated.

As the summer advanced, the threat of invasion grew, and planning and training were primarily designed to deal with it. Concentrations of barges appeared in the German-held ports across the Channel, and the RAF Bomber Command struck at them. In the phony-war days no bombs had fallen on Britain; but in August the German Luftwaffe began a systematic attack on British airfields and radar stations in an attempt to put the defending air forces out of action. The result was the Battle of Britain, a series of fierce air combats fought over the southern counties in the clear skies of summer. In these conflicts the RAF Fighter Command may be said to have inflicted on Hitler his first great defeat. The Canadian troops had front-row seats for this performance, and although as yet equipment shortages had prevented the organization of Canadian anti-aircraft artillery units, at least three infantry and engineer units claimed to have shot down German aircraft with machine-gun fire.

By early September it appeared that the invasion might come at any moment; and on the evening of the 7th (the day the Germans made their first great daylight air attack on London), GHQ Home Forces sent out the codeword 'Cromwell,' signifying that it was imminent. Next day the 7th Corps was placed on four hours' notice to move. On the 11th Churchill solemnly warned the country that the next week or so might rank with the greatest days in British history. But the invasion did not come. We now know that Hitler had fixed D-Day for 21 September, but that a week before that day he postponed it. On the 17th he postponed it indefinitely, and on 12 October the decision was announced that it would not take place before the spring. The failure to defeat the Royal Air Force had been decisive.

In Canada the Dunkirk crisis had produced a large expansion of the war effort, and the government, its earlier financial scruples forgotten, offered Britain every assistance an ill-prepared country could give. At the Admiralty's request, the four destroyers which were all the Royal Canadian Navy had immediately available were ordered across the Atlantic. The RCAF's one fully equipped fighter squadron was likewise sent to Britain, and arrived in time to take part in the late-summer battles. The British government asked for Canadian troops for Iceland, Bermuda, and Jamaica, which were promptly provided, and the 2nd Canadian Division was offered and accepted. On 17 May the government decided both to form a Canadian Corps overseas and to mobilize a 3rd Division. The rifle battalions of a 4th Division were authorized later in the month.[5]

The stage was thus set for a considerable expansion of the Canadian Army's force in Britain. A brigade of the 2nd Division had gone to Iceland, and the British government proposed that the whole division should go there. McNaughton, however, was able to prevail on Churchill to scotch this scheme. A good part of the division reached England at the beginning of August. The troops from Iceland, except for one battalion which stayed there over the winter, arrived in November, and the division's last units came in from Canada at Christmas.

Simultaneously the 7th Corps was dissolved and the Canadian Corps, likewise commanded by General McNaughton, came into existence. It fell heir to the 7th's role of 'GHQ Reserve.' The 2nd Division had moved into the barracks in the Aldershot area formerly occupied by the 1st. Through the winter, German bombing attacks on London and many other areas continued. But a great national effort had restored the equipment and organization of the army rescued from Dunkirk. As spring approached, and the invasion menace revived, the Canadian Corps was training actively for the defence of Britain; and the prospect for successful repulse of a German attack was much brighter than it had been in August and September.

To anticipate events a bit, in Ottawa during 1941 there was active discussion of the future strength and organization of the Canadian Army Overseas. The government was committed against conscription for overseas service, and apprehension of difficulty in replacing future casualties was influential. What emerged by 1942 was a plan for an overseas army of five divisions, two of them armoured, and two independent tank brigades. The 1st Army Tank Brigade went to England in June 1941, followed by the 3rd Infantry Division later that summer. The 5th Canadian Armoured Division moved overseas in the autumn. The last Canadian division to reach England was the 4th Armoured (originally raised as infantry), which crossed the ocean in the summer and autumn of 1942. The 2nd Canadian Army Tank Brigade did not go until 1943.[6] In the meantime the higher organization had been transformed. Headquarters First Canadian Army – 'first' in more senses than one – had come into existence on 6 April 1942, with Lieutenant-General McNaughton as general officer commanding-in-chief. The Canadian Corps became the 1st Canadian Corps, commanded by Lieutenant-General H.D.G. Crerar. In 1943 Headquarters 2nd Canadian Corps was organized, with Lieutenant-General E.W. Sansom as GOC.

Meanwhile the Canadian military role in England had been changing. On 22 June 1941 Hitler made the most fatal mistake of his entire career when he attacked Soviet Russia. Contrary to the expectations of the British War Office and many other Western observers, the Russians did not collapse in three weeks; on the contrary, Germany found herself committed to an eastern campaign of colossal scale to which no end could be perceived. Gradually it became clear that a German invasion of Britain was no longer probable, and the Canadian soldier there began to feel that the job to which he had seemed dedicated was fading away. However, ceaseless vigilance was still the order of things. For a time in the summer of 1941 the

Senior Officers, Canadian Army Overseas, April 1942: left to right, Lt-Gen. H.D.G. Crerar, 1st Canadian Corps; Lt-Gen. A.G.L. McNaughton, First Canadian Army; Brig. G.R. Turner; Maj.-Gen. P.J. Montague, Senior Officer, Canadian Military Headquarters, London. (DHist, DND, 6119)

2nd Canadian Division exchanged positions with a British division that had been defending part of the Sussex Coast; then in the autumn the Canadian Corps as a whole relinquished the job of GHQ Reserve and moved into Sussex. Here it came under the operational command of the general officer commanding-in-chief the British South Eastern Command. Shortly thereafter the corps was taken over by General Crerar, and the command by Lieutenant-General B.L. Montgomery. The Canadians, and Crerar, now had their first experience of this dynamic and difficult little Anglo-Irishman, of whom they were to see a good deal more.

Whatever else Montgomery was, he was a great trainer of troops; and he worked his command (he preferred to call it 'the South-Eastern Army'), and the Canadians within it, hard. He had given a taste of his quality as chief umpire in the great manœuvres called Exercise 'Bumper' at the end of September 1941, in which twelve divisions 'fought' across southern England. His own Exercise 'Tiger' (May 1942) was remembered as a classic example of tough training; McNaughton reported, 'some units marched on foot as much as 250 miles which is about the life of army boots on English roads.'[7] Montgomery also, with Crerar's concurrence, made a survey of what he called 'the Command Element in Canadian Corps'; he made adverse comments on a number of Canadian commanders, including two divisional commanders. The great majority of these men, among them the divisional commanders, Major-General G.R. Pearkes, VC, who had succeeded McNaughton at the 1st Canadian Division, and Major-General C.B. Price of the 3rd Division, were subsequently removed.[8]

These great cross-country exercises were the culminating phase of training. After Montgomery's departure for Egypt, Exercise 'Spartan' took place under the direction of GHQ Home Forces in March 1943. In it McNaughton commanded an army of six divisions, styled for exercise purposes 'Second Army' and including the extremely green 2nd Canadian Corps' headquarters as well as the experienced 1st. The Second Army's performance in these circumstances left something to be desired, and the exercise certainly did McNaughton no good in the eyes of certain British observers.[9]

By the spring of 1942 it was well over two years since the 1st Canadian Division had arrived in England, and Canadians had yet to see action. In August-September 1941 a detachment of some 500 men of the 1st Division had been employed in an expedition to the distant Arctic archipelago of Spitsbergen to disable coal-mines there, remove the Norwegian population, and deprive the Germans of meteorological information sent out by radio; but again this brought no contact with the enemy. It was common knowledge that the Canadian troops were becoming 'browned off' and that morale was suffering. General McNaughton refused to worry; his men, he was sure, knew that their time would come and were intelligent enough to wait for their moment. General Crerar was not so certain; and when he found himself the senior Canadian officer in England during a visit by McNaughton to Canada and the United States early in 1942 he used the opportunity to impress on General Montgomery, General Brooke, and Lord Louis Mountbatten (then adviser on, later chief of, Combined Operations) the desirability of giving Canadians a share in the

This German photograph of Dieppe after the battle shows German soldiers on the West Headland, overlooking the main beaches. A tank landing craft and buildings in the town are still burning, so it was probably taken on the afternoon of the raid, 19 August 1942. (DHist, DND, CN 829)

program of raiding operations being carried on against the German-held shores of the Continent.[10] This probably had some influence on the selection of a Canadian division for the raid on Dieppe on 19 August 1942.

That violent and bloody incident has been the subject of a great deal of writing,[11] and there is no point in adding to the volume of it here. It was a tactical failure, and its justification must be sought in the contribution it made to the plans for the successful invasion of Normandy in 1944. It cost the Canadian Army (mainly, the 2nd Canadian Infantry Division) 3367 casualties, of which 907 were fatal, out of a force engaged of roughly 5000 men. The effect was in every way traumatic. It made the Canadians (and other people too) realize just how difficult the task of defeating Germany was going to be. The 2nd Canadian Division had to be rebuilt and retrained before it could again take its place in the order of battle.

The raid could not itself be called one of the turning-points of the war; but it came at a moment when the tide was turning. The previous December had brought Pearl Harbor and catapulted the United States into the war. The presence of a few American Rangers at Dieppe was symbolic of the way the balance of forces was changing. A few months later came Montgomery's victory in North Africa at Alamein; early in 1943 the German Sixth Army surrendered to the Russians at Stalingrad. The initiative now rested with the Allies.

The Canadian government was becoming aware of a powerful popular demand that its military force, so long 'idle' in England, should get into action, and it was prepared to overrule McNaughton on this question. In the spring of 1943 it brought pressure to bear on Churchill to employ a Canadian division in the next stage of operations in the Mediterranean; and in consequence the 1st Canadian Division was substituted for the 3rd British Division in the planned assault on Sicily.[12] It was commanded by Major-General G.G. Simonds, for Major-General H.L.N. Salmon, who had succeeded Pearkes, was killed in an air crash during the period of planning.

Thus it was that in July 1943, more than three-and-a-half years after it landed in England, the 1st Canadian Division went into action against the Germans, as part of General Montgomery's Eighth Army. The 1st Canadian Army Tank Brigade went with it. They gave a good account of themselves, and Simonds made a favourable impression on Montgomery, who thereafter regarded Guy Simonds as one of his own. McNaughton had vainly hoped that the division would return to England after Sicily to give First Canadian Army the benefit of its battle experience. People in Ottawa had other ideas. They preferred to think of building the Canadian force in the Mediterranean up to a corps, sending out the 5th Armoured Division and the 1st Corps headquarters and corps troops under General Crerar. Though the Allied command in that theatre was far from enthusiastic, politics prevailed and the troops moved in the autumn of 1943. All this was contrary to the views of General McNaughton, who had no desire to see the First Canadian Army broken up. Simultaneously the British military authorities, declaring that they thought McNaughton unsuited to command an army in operations, were able to take advantage of his quarrel with his own government, and he was forced out of the army command, to be replaced in

Canadian Bren carriers pass through a southern English village on the eve of the
Normandy D-Day, May 1944. The censor has blacked out the formation sign on the leading vehicle.
(Harold G. Aikman, PAC, PA 154974)

A Canadian anti-tank gun in action during the desperate battle with German paratroopers for the Italian Adriatic town of Ortona, December 1943. (Terry F. Rowe, PAC / DND, PA 141671)

Canadian armour in Operation 'Tractable,' the breakout
from the Normandy bridgehead, 14 August 1944. (Lt D.I. Grant, PAC / DND, PA 116525)

due time by Crerar, who returned from Italy in March 1944.[13]

The politics that had consigned the 1st Canadian Corps to the 'spaghetti league' condemned its soldiers to take part in the long and bitter advance of the Allied armies up the Italian boot. The 1st Division crossed the Straits of Messina into Italy proper in September 1943, and fought its way forward with the rest of the Eighth Army until December, when it was involved in the costly battle on the Moro River and the capture of Ortona in a week of sanguinary street-fighting. The 1st Canadian Corps (now commanded by Lieutenant-General E.L.M. Burns) fought its first battle as a corps in the attack on the Adolf Hitler Line across the Liri Valley in May 1944.

Up the Adriatic coast the slow struggle continued. The corps played an eminent part in the breaking of the Gothic Line at the beginning of September; but here, and in the advance to Rimini that followed, it paid a heavy price for victory. At the end of the year the Canadians, whose commander now was Lieutenant-General Charles Foulkes, had reached the limit of their long march in Italy, on the River Senio. Their government, long regretting its earlier error, had been seeking to have the 1st Canadian Corps return to its proper place in the First Canadian Army in Northwest Europe. Allied strategy now permitted this, and the movement began in February 1945. Some 93,000 Canadian soldiers had served in Italy, and they had suffered 26,000 casualties, of which 5764 were fatal.[14]

The movement of the 1st Corps to Italy had left only three Canadian divisions serving in England, and the 1st and 5th would have to be replaced in the First Canadian Army by British and Allied formations, which would serve under Canadian command just as the 1st Canadian Corps served under the Eighth British Army in Italy. The crisis of the war in the west was approaching; the Allies had been developing their plan for Operation 'Overlord,' the liberation of Northwest Europe.* General Dwight D. Eisenhower, the American officer who had been in supreme command in the Mediterranean, came to England to command the Allied Expeditionary Force; General Montgomery likewise came back to command the British army group for the invasion and, in the initial phase, all the ground forces. Major-General Simonds, promoted to lieutenant-general, was appointed to the 2nd Canadian Corps. General Crerar's Canadian Army, the final plan provided, would be in reserve during the assault phase; but one Canadian division, the 3rd, under Major-General R.F.L. Keller, would take part in the assault under a British corps, along with the 2nd Canadian Army Tank Brigade, now rechristened the 2nd Armoured Brigade.

The cross-Channel attack was regarded as an extremely perilous enterprise, not least by those who remembered Dieppe. The German defences were formidable; the men who manned them, as it proved, even more so. Prime Minister Mackenzie King during the Quebec Conference of 1943 recorded in his diary, 'The more of our men participate in the campaign in Italy, the fewer there are likely to be who will be involved in the crossing of the Channel which, as Churchill says, will be a very tough business.'[15] This is clearly why he,

---

*'Overlord' ended only with the German surrender in May 1945. The assault phase, the landings in Normandy, was termed Operation 'Neptune.'

Men of Les Fusiliers Mont-Royal flush out Germans
in Groningen, the Netherlands, 15 April 1945.
(Lt. D. Guravitch, PAC / DND, PA 130964)

rather reluctantly, sided against McNaughton in the argument over breaking up the army. The soldiers of the assault force were well aware that it was going to be a tough business; the British media lost no opportunity of reminding them.

The business began on 6 June 1944, on the beaches of Normandy. The 3rd Canadian Division did their work and took their losses, with the other Allied formations; and as the bloody summer campaign proceeded they were followed into action by the 2nd Infantry Division and the 4th Armoured. Few Canadians now remained in the English counties that had known them so long; they were finally doing the unpleasant job that had brought them across the sea. The 2nd Canadian Corps took over a sector of the Normandy front on 11 July, the First Canadian Army on 23 July. In the desperate fighting that followed, culminating in the near-destruction of two German armies in the 'Falaise Gap,' Canadian infantry casualties were so heavy that they brought on a political crisis in Canada in the autumn and forced the government to send conscripts overseas. For the rest of the eleven-month campaign, Crerar's army was on the extreme left of the Allied line. After its share in the Normandy victory it pushed on up the Channel, clearing the German coastal fortresses, Le Havre (which fell to the 1st British Corps), Boulogne, and Calais.

October brought the Battle of the Scheldt, when the Canadian Army had a grim struggle to open the vital port of Antwerp, essential to supply an Allied thrust into Germany. In February 1945 that thrust was launched in earnest, when Crerar's army (reinforced with many British divisions) had the task of clearing the area between the Maas and the Rhine. By

10 March the Germans had been pushed across their great river, and the Americans had already got a foothold beyond it. On 23 March the main attack across the Rhine was launched on the British front, Canadians playing a part; now First Canadian Army began its liberating advance through the Eastern Netherlands. The 2nd Canadian Corps pushed on towards the North Sea. The 1st Corps, fresh from Italy, moved in on the left; late in April they were confronting the Germans on what was called the Grebbe Line, when what amounted to a truce came into effect here while food supplies were moved into the occupied area to succour the starving Dutch. On the 2nd Corps' front fierce if rather disorganized resistance was still being encountered up to the moment of the German surrender to General Montgomery on Lüneburg Heath on 4 May. Hostilities on the British front ended officially on the morning of 5 May.[16]

The operations beginning on the Normandy D-Day had cost the Canadian Army 44,339 casualties; in them 11,336 Canadian officers and men had given their lives. Many of them were mourned in English towns and villages as well as in the distant communities from which they came.

The Royal Canadian Air Force overseas was very closely – indeed, inextricably – involved with Britain's Royal Air Force. This was largely the result of the British Commonwealth Air Training Plan, which was set up immediately after the outbreak of war. This great scheme centring in Canada ultimately produced 131,000 aircrew, of whom 73,000 were Canadian and 42,000 British; the rest came from Australia and New Zealand.[17] It was frankly said by Canadian ministers during the difficult negotiations over the plan in 1939 that it was a recruiting scheme for the RAF,[18] and in practice this was largely true. The original agreement specified that except for men required for the home defence squadrons of the RCAF, all Canadian aircrew produced by the scheme should be 'placed at the disposal of the Government of the United Kingdom,' subject to arrangements being made to identify them as Canadian, either by organizing them in distinctive units or otherwise. As the war proceeded, RCAF units were organized overseas in increasing numbers; at the end, forty-eight RCAF squadrons were serving in overseas theatres. Yet even now more Canadians were in RAF than in RCAF units: in August 1944, about 17,000 as against 10,000.

Three RCAF squadrons went overseas from Canada in 1940. One, No 1 (later 401) Fighter Squadron, then Canada's only effective fighter unit, was ordered to England in May in answer to an urgent British call for help. It arrived, we have seen, in time to play a part in the Battle of Britain, being credited with thirty-one enemy aircraft destroyed and forty-three probably destroyed or damaged.[19] Beginning in 1941, further RCAF squadrons were formed overseas, and Air Training Plan graduates began to arrive in England late in 1940, most of them going to RAF units. From this time on the RCAF had an increasing role in Royal Air Force operations based on Britain. In August 1942 eight RCAF squadrons (and a considerable but unknown number of Canadians in RAF units) formed part of the air umbrella that covered the army and naval forces that carried out the raid on Dieppe.

Canadian Spitfires over England: aircraft of No 403 (Wolf) Squadron, RCAF, based at Kenley, south of London, 1943. (PAC / DND, PA 115117)

At the beginning of 1943 No 6 (RCAF) Bomber Group of the RAF Bomber Command came into existence. This, the only air vice-marshal's active command in the RCAF overseas, was commanded in the first instance by Air Vice-Marshal G.E. Brookes and subsequently by Air Vice-Marshal C.M. ('Black Mike') McEwen. Its final strength was fourteen squadrons. Its headquarters was at Allerton Hall, west of York, and its bases were scattered across the North Riding of Yorkshire and the southern edge of Durham.[20] From them its bombers went out, night after night, against the cities of Germany. It was desperately dangerous work; and 9913 Canadians lost their lives serving in Bomber Command, either in No 6 Group or in RAF squadrons.[21] The command's total death roll was 55,888, of whom 4037 came from the Royal Australian Air Force and 1676 from the Royal New Zealand Air Force. Other dominions, including South Africa, lost sixty-one, and the Poles and other allies, 1402. But the heaviest toll still fell upon the United Kingdom: 38,462.[22]

Not all senior RAF officers appreciated the help their service got from the dominions. Sir Arthur ('Bomber') Harris, commander-in-chief of Bomber Command, wrote at least twice to the Air Ministry protesting against the increase of 'Foreign and Dominion' elements in the RAF and in his own command. In 1943 he complained that over half his aircrew were 'already of non-UK identity.' Nobody at the Air Ministry pointed out to him that without the 'Foreign and Dominion' people the RAF could hardly have retained its status as a major force in Allied air power.[23]

The fighter forces of the RCAF overseas came to be chiefly concentrated in the RAF's 2nd Tactical Air Force, which co-operated with Field-Marshal Montgomery's 21st Army Group in the Northwest Europe campaign. The Canadian squadrons formed three Spitfire wings, a Typhoon wing, and a reconnaissance wing, all incorporated in No 83 Group of the 2nd TAF, which, though a little more than half Canadian in composition, had a British headquarters. Rather curiously, No 83 supported the Second British Army, while the all-British No 84 Group was assigned to the First Canadian Army. The Canadian wings were active in the destruction visited upon the German armies attempting to escape through the Falaise Gap in August 1944, and continued to play a leading part in support of the Allied advance through the Low Countries into Germany. RCAF fighters destroyed at least thirty-six enemy aircraft on New Year's Day 1945, when the Luftwaffe rallied its dwindling forces for the famous 'hangover raid' on Allied airfields.

RCAF squadrons also served in Coastal Command, killing many German submarines; one fighter squadron distinguished itself in the Desert Air Force, in North Africa and later in Italy;* and three squadrons worked in the RAF Transport Command, two of them in the Far East. One coastal squadron was based in Ceylon in 1942–4. There were three air observation post squadrons, flown by officers of the Royal Canadian Artillery and having the task of spotting for guns on the ground. Finally, one must once more recall the thousands of

---

*It was a curious experience, on a cold wet spring day in Italy, to pass a sign directing travellers to 'Headquarters, Desert Air Force.'

Twin-engined Wellington bombers of No 405 Squadron, RCAF, the first Canadian
bomber squadron overseas, being 'bombed up' at Pocklington, Yorkshire, in 1941. (RCAF, PL 4501)

A Canadian motor torpedo boat at speed. Two Canadian motor torpedo-boat flotillas
were actively engaged against German forces in the English Channel in 1944. (PAC / DND, PA 144587)

The Canadian corvette *Battleford* guards the port side of an
Atlantic convoy that stretches to the far horizon, November 1941. (PAC / DND, PA 115353)

more or less anonymous Canadians who served around the world in the units of the Royal Air Force. Wherever the RAF was found, there too were Canadian airmen serving in its units and wearing the badge of Canada.

The peculiarly intimate relationship of the RCAF with the RAF presents special problems for the Canadian historian. The people writing the official history of the RCAF have found many of their sources in London, but some information required is simply not to be found anywhere.

The Royal Canadian Navy served in many seas and had shore establishments in several countries. In the beginning its small force of destroyers worked in Canadian and adjoining waters, protecting convoys and merchant vessels generally from a submarine menace which had not yet appeared on the North American coasts. In May 1940, faced with the crisis resulting from the fall of France and a desperate shortage of destroyers, the British government asked that the Canadian vessels should be sent to join the battle being fought around the British Isles, and Canada dispatched them at once. For the next period of the war her main naval force worked in British waters, first in operations in and near the English Channel, subsequently in convoy protection as part of the Clyde Escort Force.[24] In 1941 the westward extension of enemy submarine activity led to the establishment of St John's, Newfoundland, as an escort base, and for some time the Canadian naval effort was concentrated in a Newfoundland Escort Force, whose task was escorting convoys between Halifax and a point south of Iceland, where escorts from the United Kingdom took over. After April 1942 the system was changed; a Western Local Escort Force based at Halifax took the convoys as far as a meeting point east of St John's, and thence the Mid-Ocean Escort Force, increasingly composed of RCN escort groups, took up the task for the whole voyage to Londonderry in Northern Ireland, a port with which Canadians became familiar.

The Battle of the Atlantic involved fighting North Atlantic storms as well as Admiral Dönitz's wolf-packs of U-boats. The RCN had undergone enormous expansion, in numbers both of ships and personnel; the Canadians who fought the battle were largely amateurs, still learning as they fought, and for a long time their ships were not as well equipped for anti-submarine warfare as those of the Royal Navy. Yet they carried a large part of the burden of the fight, and it certainly could not have been won without them. This contribution was belatedly recognized in March 1943 by the organization of the Canadian Northwest Atlantic command, which placed escort operations in the ocean sector adjacent to Canada under a Canadian officer, Rear-Admiral L.W. Murray. Canadian ships, alone or in co-operation with other ships and aircraft, destroyed twenty-seven U-boats in all. Only a minority of these were sunk on the main Atlantic convoy route; other kills were made as far away as the Mediterranean, the Faeroe Islands, and the Caribbean.[25]

Many tasks apart from convoy escort fell to the RCN. Numbers of officers and men were loaned to the Royal Navy – some 2400 at the peak.[26] Canadians manned landing craft in European waters, serving in the amphibious operations at Dieppe, North Africa, and Sicily. Sixteen Canadian corvettes took part in the North African landings of November 1942. And a large contribution was made to the Normandy invasion of June 1944 and the operations subsidiary to it: it is reckoned that some 110 vessels and 10,000 men were involved. Canadian destroyers fought two fierce battles in the chops of the Channel in April 1944.

In the nature of things, Canadian sailors saw less of the United Kingdom than soldiers and airmen. They were birds of passage, normally seen in British towns only during brief periods of shore leave when their ships were working in British waters or at the end of a convoy run. It was found necessary, however, to maintain a manning and pay depot in Britain, which finally was established at Greenock under the name HMCS *Niobe*; and a growing establishment in London maintained liaison, including technical liaison, with the British Admiralty.[27]

In all its varied operations, the Royal Canadian Navy suffered 1797 fatal casualties.

CHAPTER TWO

Getting Acquainted

HEN THE LEADING TROOPS of the 1st Canadian Division landed in England in December 1939, two quite dissimilar societies came into contact. What sort of people were the young men who filled the ranks of the two Canadian divisions mobilized in September of that year? The strength of the Permanent Force, Canada's little regular army, was only a trifle over 4000 officers and men. Beyond this there was the citizen militia; beyond that, the man in the street. Everybody joining the new 'Canadian Active Service Force' was a volunteer. The militia regiments ordered to mobilize naturally looked first to their own peacetime members. Thus in Toronto the Royal Regiment of Canada, a good militia infantry unit slated for the 2nd Division, held a mobilization parade on 2 September and called for men for its Active Service Force battalion. Of thirty officers on parade, twenty-nine volunteered; of 251 other ranks, 156 came forward. Few units recorded their members' performance this way; but it is doubtful whether many did better. Since the unit was to have a war strength of 774 other ranks, 618 men were needed from the general public. A recruiting station was opened, and by 19 September the battalion was at full strength.[1]

It is not easy to characterize the men who, during this fortnight or so, enlisted in Canada's first two overseas divisions. We know that, during the month of September, 54,844 Canadians (not counting officer appointments) 'joined the colours'; no other month of the long war saw so many enlistments.[2] Who were these now faceless men? Official records afford no way of breaking down the statistics, and we are left to speculate. Canada during the past few years had passed through much the same mental struggle as Britain, as her people watched the progress of Adolf Hitler's cynical aggression in Europe; gradually a pacific and unmilitary society had been brought to the point where it was prepared, however reluctantly, to take up arms in defence of freedom. Of the men who joined the forces in 1939, many no doubt were moved by anger against Nazi brutality. Many were idealists and patriots, fired by inherited memories of the legendary Canadian Corps of 1914–18, and moved also by the ancestral link to Great Britain, now once more fighting for her life. These men were grimly doing what they saw as their duty. Nowhere, it is fair to say, was any voice heard echoing Rupert Brooke's: 'Now, God be thanked Who has matched us with His hour.' That was the voice of 1914. This was 1939.

Men who joined the forces later sometimes said that the often ill-behaved recruits of 1939 were simply unemployed people who joined to get off the streets. The unemployment situation in Canada is worth examining. The Great Depression that had followed the stock market crash of 1929 was long past its worst, but many would-be workers were still without jobs. According to the *Canada Year Book*, the estimated total of wage-earners unemployed in September 1939 was 306,000 (at the worst point, in 1933, its figure was 646,000).[3] These statistics are, to say the least, very conservative. But there were certainly plenty of men to whom regular if small pay, army rations, sound boots, and a warm suit of the new battle-dress must have seemed attractive. Just how many of these enlisted in the 1st and 2nd Canadian divisions is anybody's guess. One thing is certain. It was a very mixed body of citizens who signed the attestation papers in September 1939: many potential heroes at one end of the scale, and doubtless the occasional petty criminal at the other.*

The 1st Division on its arrival in England found itself quartered in and around Aldershot in Hampshire, Britain's largest peacetime military station. The British War Office

*In June 1941, when personnel selection procedures were being planned, it was reported that of 2153 overseas medical boards which had recommended men for return to Canada, 453 concerned mental cases, including thirty-six of 'psychopathic personality.' The opinion was expressed that 'a large proportion were mentally unstable before enlistment.'[4]

doubtless thought it was conferring a kindness on the Canadians in making over to them the permanent barracks of Aldershot, a marked contrast with the procedure of 1914 when the First Canadian Contingent spent a too-famous winter on Salisbury Plain, largely under canvas. The Canadians did not appreciate this consideration. The Aldershot barracks, some of them dating back to mid-Victorian days, were uncomfortable by Canadian standards, and of course none of them had central heating. Moreover, the people of Aldershot and the neighbouring communities had been accustomed to the presence of soldiers since the Crimean War, and regarded them as permanent but not necessarily attractive features of the landscape. They were unlikely to show particular enthusiasm for new tenants of the barracks merely because they happened to come from across the Atlantic.

Nevertheless, there were plenty of hospitable people in Aldershot and the nearby places. They quickly set up a Dominion Hospitality Centre in Aldershot, which arranged for local residents to entertain soldiers in their homes and also helped with advice about weekend or longer leaves and a great variety of other matters. A little later a similar establishment was organized in Bordon, a few miles away, and was soon assisting about thirty men a day. 'Private hospitality,' it recorded, 'is, of course, in the greatest demand, but ... we have been called on many times to make hotel reservations for the officers and Overseas Club reservations for other ranks.' In general, these services were certainly much appreciated; but truth compels one to note a Canadian record that there were occasional complaints that soldiers did not arrive when a family meal had been arranged for them or that they arrived drunk or borrowed money from their hostesses.[5]

It would certainly be unfair to blame the people of the Aldershot area for the difficulties that arose with the Canadians during their first months in those parts, and which gave the Canadians a bad name with some English people. As we have said, the 1st Canadian Division was almost wholly untrained when it landed in England and its men were in great part strangers to discipline; after all, most of them had been civilians three or four months before, and they were still not much more than civilians in uniform. The Canadian formations that came in later, including the 2nd Division, had undergone varying periods of military life and discipline in Canada and were more like the soldiers Aldershot was used to. In the meantime, there were problems.

The Canada from which these young men had come was in many ways widely different from the England into which they had suddenly been catapulted. English society was, to use a modern word, more 'permissive.' In particular, it was more permissive in the matter of drink. The English public-house, so agreeably celebrated in the writings of P.G. Wodehouse, was an institution with which few Canadians were acquainted. Canada, it is true, had always been a hard-drinking country, and it was the hard drinking that produced the prohibition movement, which scored its great triumphs during the First World War. Enforced temperance was then represented as a war-winning measure, and from 1915 every Canadian province except predominantly French Quebec enacted legislation outlawing the public sale of alcoholic beverages. Explaining the Ontario Temperance Act to the Ontario legislature in 1916, Premier William Hearst exhorted members to avoid the path taken in Britain, where the government had admitted that it was 'impotent to remove the evil.' In Russia, he said, stopping the sale of vodka had 'strengthened the nation and enabled the Russians to play a heroic part.'

It was a long time before Canada rid itself of prohibition; in 1927 it was replaced in Ontario by a system of government control of sale, but to consume alcohol in public was still illegal. By the outbreak of the second war, Ontario (from which incidentally between a third and a half of the Canadian volunteers came) had progressed to the point of having what were officially called 'beverage rooms,' repulsive establishments in which beer (but nothing else) could be drunk and music and any other form of entertainment were banned. Other provinces had moved, or were moving, in the same direction.[6]

To the unsophisticated young Canadian soldier, a place where men, and even women, could meet (within certain permitted hours) to drink freely what they chose and enjoy themselves, a place known as the 'poor man's club,' was a novel experience. Much could be written about the impact of the British pub on the Canadian serviceman, and vice versa. One long-term effect was felt in Canada in later years: the prevalence of establishments that strive to convince the public that they are, or are similar to, British pubs. In the short term the young 'colonials' new to England certainly tended to drink too much, and to get into trouble. People in Hampshire and Surrey towns in 1940 complained that in the evenings the

Increasingly as the war went on the local pub was a centre of pleasant contact between the Canadians and the English. In this picture taken in May 1945 cheerfulness is undoubtedly helped along by the fact that the war is over. (Arthur L. Cole, PAC / DND, PA 154975)

streets were full of drunken and profane Canadians noisily making their way back to the barracks which they found so disagreeable.

The weather is an important part of the story. In wartime England the weather was a military secret. Meteorological information was too useful to the enemy to allow it to be given in the newspapers at the time (the last forecast published before such things vanished from the press in September 1939 is said to have been, 'Further outlook: unsettled'). But when, after the passage of a suitable number of weeks, the London *Times* was permitted to refer to the question, it revealed that the winter of 1939–40 had witnessed 'the coldest conditions since 1894.' The Canadians in the Aldershot barracks, very inadequately heated by a few open fireplaces, froze and complained; they did not realize that they were being given a larger allowance of coal than British troops.[7] Major-General George Kitching, then a subaltern in the Royal Canadian Regiment, recalls that park benches and seats at bus stops disappeared; they were being broken up to serve as fuel to heat Canadian barrack-rooms, thereby making a further contribution to Canadian unpopularity.

The effect of bad weather was magnified by one of the great torments of English wartime life: the blackout. Nobody who has not experienced it can fully appreciate the misery of life in a country deprived of normal modern street lighting and plunged at nightfall into more-than-medieval darkness. In the Middle Ages the wayfarer could at least be cheered by a glimpse of firelight from a cottage window; even this was illegal in England in 1939–45. The blackout was literally a major horror of the war. Its effect was mitigated by the fact that summer (daylight-saving) time was in effect throughout the year, with double (two hours) summer time in the summer months; but as winter came on the advance of blackout-time was a grim fact of life.

Vehicle lights were reduced to mere slits, and driving, or walking on streets and roads, became dangerous pursuits. Many a Canadian was maimed or killed in night vehicle accidents. Motorcycle dispatch riders had a particularly dangerous trade; men spoke grimly of Brookwood Cemetery as 'the DRs' holding unit.' People in well-lighted Canada found it hard to believe stories of persons in blacked-out railway stations getting out of a train compartment on the wrong side, expecting to step on to the platform, and instead crashing down on to the line in a perhaps near-fatal fall. And, of course, all criminal or illegitimate activities, including those connected with sex, were facilitated by the pervading darkness. Almost anything could happen in the blackout, and a great deal did.

At the end of the war the British government, after some encouragement from Canada, decided to institute a medal – the Defence Medal – to recognize service in defence of areas which, while not scenes of actual operations, were closely threatened or subjected to heavy air attacks; this obviously meant, primarily, the United Kingdom. The ribbon for this medal, it was said, was designed by King George VI. At either end was a green stripe, representing 'England's green and pleasant land,' which such great numbers of Canadians had come to know, and, it is fair to say, in many cases to love. In the centre was a broad area of orange, representing the flames of the Blitz, of which Canadians had seen more than enough. And through the green ran two narrow lines of sable black. They stood for the blackout. Every Canadian who was there would agree that that should not be forgotten.

In the cold winter of 1939–40 the Blitz was still in the future. Britain and France were still fighting the phony war. Hitler, having destroyed Poland, hoped that Britain and France might now be foolish enough to make peace, and refrained from action against them by land or air. On the Continent the Allied and German armies lay quiet, watching each other. In Hampshire and Surrey there was no evident menace, no bombs were falling, and when rude young Englishmen sometimes asked the Canadians what they were doing there it was not entirely easy to find an answer. Most of them certainly wished they were back home.

Just how bad the situation was is made clear in a report by British postal censors on a batch of Canadian army mail examined in February 1940 (it had been agreed that all censorship in the United Kingdom was the responsibility of the British authorities). The report ran in part:

Boredom, homesickness and a feeling of not being really needed appear to be the main reasons why nearly all these Canadian soldiers grumble. The majority of the writers warn their friends and relatives not to join the Army.

The recent bad weather has made them dislike this country considerably ...

The insufficiency and bad quality of the food annoys the majority of the writers.

Commenting on this grim recital, General Crerar wrote to the deputy chief postal censor that the Canadians should be in much better spirits with the coming of better weather.[8] This proved a true prophecy, the more so as the spring weather coincided with the end of the phony war, signalled in the first instance by the German invasion of Denmark and Norway in April. In May bombs began to fall on Britain, and the Western Front exploded into violent action. Thereafter soldiers and civilians alike viewed the situation with different eyes.

The move of Canadian Force to the Northampton area late in May (above, page 7) was a turning-point in the Canadians' relations with their British hosts. The people of Northamptonshire were less sated with the presence of soldiery than those of Aldershot; and perhaps the fact that this was the week of Dunkirk had its influence. At any rate, they took McNaughton's men to their hearts in a way that the Canadians never forgot. Practically every unit war diary commented on the warmth of the welcome; one noted that 'meal parades were very small'[9] – the local people were inviting the troops to eat with them in their homes. The Hastings and Prince Edward Regiment found itself in the village of Finedon, and its historian records that during its brief sojourn there 'a love of England which became a part of almost every man took root.' 'Finedon brought the unit its first unobstructed view of England. It was a view that memory harbours still.'[10]

Nevertheless, an instantaneous miracle had not been worked, and there were still troubles ahead. A month later, after the aborted expedition to France with the 'Second BEF,' the stay of Canadian Force in the Oxford area was not so pleasant as the

A near miss at Canadian Military Headquarters, London, when a bomb fell
near the back door of the Sun Life Building, Pall Mall East, October 1940. (DHist, DND, P2–11)

The London Home Guard provided the 'enemy' for the 48th Highlanders
of Canada in this exercise among the ruins, July 1941. (L.A. Audrain, PAC / DND, PA 147106)

one around Northampton. The evidence is a letter which a member of the editorial staff of the London *Daily Express*, Peter Howard (noted as a leader of the Moral Rearmament movement), sent to his paper's general manager about 1 July. A copy was sent to Mike Pearson, the official secretary at Canada House (Mike knew everybody):

The best story from Oxford is the conduct of the Canadians who are there in force. They are becoming really disliked by the population as well as by the British soldiers and the military police. From personal observation I can testify that they are really a little extreme in their pleasures. There were hundreds of them around the streets last evening, and without exaggeration half of them were drunk. They were yelling like redskins, breaking a certain amount of glass etc., and grabbing hold of the women. They were driving their military vans fast and recklessly and I was told they have had several accidents ... It is a shame that something cannot be done to put this thing right. For the Canadians are grand people, and if they could be induced to moderate their behaviour just a little they would make a tremendous number of friends in Oxford, instead of which all the people I met were counting the days to their departure.[11]

That Howard was not inventing is evidenced by the war diary of the 1st Canadian Provost Company, which records that on 29 June two of its officers interviewed the Chief of the Oxford city police, who asked that details from the company be placed on duty there in the evenings. (Had the Provost been more experienced, this might have been done earlier.) Twelve men under a sergeant were accordingly sent in that night. 'The town of Oxford was very congested with Canadian soldiers and many under the influence of drink.' Five men were arrested by the Provost and placed in city police cells to await unit escorts; 'it was after midnight before the town was quiet.'

Pearson passed Howard's letter on to the Canadian military authorities, and on 8 July divisional headquarters circulated copies to formation and unit commanders confidentially, expressing the opinion that the trouble was caused by 'a relatively few individuals who abused the freedom it was sought to give them to the maximum extent possible,' and directing that 'cases of drunkenness and disorderly conduct are in future to be dealt with severely.'[12] Something can be forgiven to men who had suffered so many disappointments and frustrations, but the contrast with the good relations established in Northampton is painful.

Why the difference? Conditions were not the same. The troops at Northampton were billeted in the towns and villages, in immediate contact with the people. The Royal Canadian Regiment's diarist actually wrote, 'The civilians were most hurt if troops were not billeted with them.'[13] At Oxford the units were distributed under canvas in the country for miles around; Oxford was just the neighbouring town, the place where one sought amusement – and booze. They had no chance to meet the people as friends. This may not excuse the Canadians' behaviour, but it helps to explain it.

Beginning in this summer of 1940 Canadian servicemen shared with British civilians the experience of heavy and sometimes constant bombing by the enemy. Increasing numbers of them were engaged in the reciprocal bombing of

Germany. All war is barbarous; but the deliberate bombing of civilian communities, which was practised by both sides equally in this war, is warfare of an unusually barbarous kind.

Deadly for the bombed, it was deadly also for the bombers. The Mackenzie King government's acceptance of the British Commonwealth Air Training Plan resulted in great numbers of young Canadians being incorporated into Britain's Royal Air Force, and in particular into the RAF Bomber Command. The bombing of Germany was the most lethal of all the tasks that fell to British forces in the Second World War; nearly a quarter of the three Canadian services' whole death-toll died in Bomber Command.[14] The grim experience of these aircrews, based in Britain, and setting out night after night across the North Sea on their appallingly perilous missions, is described by Murray Peden of Winnipeg in *A Thousand Shall Fall*, one of the best personal books about the war that has been written anywhere.

The German air attack directed against the population of Britain may be said to have begun in earnest with the assault on London on 7 September 1940. It went on, in one form or another, throughout the war, London being the chief target but many other towns and cities also being heavily hit. But what is remembered as the Blitz proper may be said to have ended with the savage blow at the capital on the night of 10 May 1941, which was followed by a lull as the Luftwaffe prepared for, and later engaged in, the ultimately disastrous campaign against Russia. That lull was in part responsible for the almost hysterical adulation of Soviet Russia in Britain thereafter, which those who were there have no difficulty in understanding.

The shared experience of the Blitz, and the Canadians' warm admiration of how the people of London and the rest of the country 'took it,' did a great deal to bring Canadians and Britons together. The atmosphere now was utterly different from the days of the phony war. No one could doubt that there was a war on, everyone was in it together, and helpers from across the sea assumed more of the aspect of friends in need.

The Canadians closest to the front line of the Blitz were those at the army's administrative headquarters, Canadian Military Headquarters, London, situated in the Sun Life Building in Cockspur Street, next to Canada House. The building was never actually hit, but on 11 October it had a miss so near that the blast blew in windows and put elevators and the heating system out of action for some time. Nobody was killed while on duty in the building, but the staff suffered casualties in their quarters or elsewhere. Soldiers in London on leave were sometimes killed or wounded. When a bomb hit the Café de Paris in Coventry Street, near Leicester Square, on the night of 8–9 March 1941, four Canadians were among the dead, two of them non-commissioned officers of CMHQ.

As with all such establishments, the staff of CMHQ grew and grew. By the end of the German war it amounted to 3328 military personnel and 745 civilians, the latter mainly British.[15] Except for the members of the Canadian Women's Army Corps, the military staff did not live in army quarters but were 'on subsistence'; that is, they were paid an allowance and found their own places to live, taking their chances with the civilians in the lottery of whose house was hit or spared, who lived or died. For them, as for millions of civilians, bombing became a

On guard against tip-and-run raiders, a 40-millimetre Bofors anti-aircraft gun has the Grand Hotel, Brighton, for a background, March 1943. (A.M. Stirton, PAC / DND, PA 154973)

way of life; you got used to it. The siren went. Usually, after the earliest days, it was a minor raid, with some distant thudding of bombs and the crack of anti-aircraft guns, followed shortly perhaps by the All Clear. Sometimes it was the beginning of a long bad night, which at best meant little sleep, and at worst meant that the morning found you homeless, or even dead. But life went on; the big red buses ran, though their progress might be slowed or their routes diverted by bomb damage; the tube trains sped along, though the station platforms were blocked by the recumbent forms of sleeping shelterers. The London theatres were all closed by the first big Blitz, except for the indomitable little Windmill, but by the end of 1940 they were coming back into operation, with curtain times adapted to battle conditions. Donald Wolfit was doing 'lunchtime Shakespeare.' From the units in the field, Canadian officers and men continued to pour into London in search of recreation.

In April 1941 there were two big raids which Londoners always spoke of as 'the Wednesday and the Saturday' (the 16th and the 19th). The first of these attacks was particularly serious for the Canadian Army, which lost twenty-two men killed, ten of them in the destruction of the Victoria League Club in Malet Street, one of the many British establishments that provided accommodation for servicemen on leave. CMHQ had five fatal casualties. Gunner Jack Chambers of the Royal Canadian Horse Artillery won the George Medal for rescuing a fireman from the burning wreck of an Auxiliary Fire Service pump that had been hit in Beckenham in southeastern London. The raid of the night of 10–11 May, the last attack of this period on London, was singularly destructive; it was on this night that the

An English farmer, his sheep, and his ducks seem unperturbed by the presence among them of a Canadian gun-crew with their 2-pounder anti-tank gun. (DHist, DND, 10–13)

House of Commons chamber was wrecked. Four Canadian soldiers were killed in this raid.

In general, the rural areas where most of the Canadian military units were stationed had little interest for the Luftwaffe; but even here bombs fell. In November 1940 Headquarters 7th Corps recorded receiving a message from Eastern Command authorizing the use of troops to help farmers fill bomb craters in their fields. The corps diarist recorded, 'This is little enough to ask of the Army and certainly no more than the civilian might reasonably expect at this time yet the War Office have hedged the offer with various financial requirements entailing a great deal of irritating and irksome work in units.'[16] Sometimes there were much more dangerous tasks. On 21 September an attack on the Hawker aircraft factory in Weybridge, Surrey, left an unexploded 500-pound bomb lying outside one of the buildings. 'A' Company of No 1 Pioneer Battalion, Royal Canadian Engineers, was working nearby, repairing a plant damaged in an earlier attack. It was asked whether it could produce a bomb-disposal squad. It could not; but it did produce two bold young officers, Captain D.W. Cunnington and Lieutenant J.M.S. Patton, who with the help of some courageous Home Guards rolled the bomb on to a piece of corrugated iron. This they towed away behind a truck to a safe spot where, some hours later, it exploded harmlessly. Patton received the George Cross and Cunnington the George Medal.[17]

Many provincial cities suffered heavily from bombing; but this seldom affected the Canadians directly. An exception was the great port of Liverpool, which had bad raids in November and December 1940 and again in March and April 1941, and then in May 1941, just before the lull, had seven successive nights of bombing. A Canadian unit was involved here, for in March 1941 the Canadian Transit Depot, staffed by the Lorne Scots, was moved to Liverpool to be near a principal port of landing and departure. The Scots at the Seaforth Barracks were in the midst of the big week in May. Their own quarters were knocked about, but they and the men awaiting return to Canada (many of them of low medical category) laboured at the work of rescuing the unfortunate civilians of the district amid scenes which one Canadian wrote would have made Dante's *Inferno* seem 'pale and colourless.' Captain D.C. Heggie, the depot's medical officer, won the George Medal on the night of 3–4 May for the courage with which he went about the business of succouring people trapped in the ruins of demolished buildings. Three nights later, when a parachute mine landed near his first-aid post, he was injured in the head, and, still working to help other casualties, was forced by loss of blood to accept evacuation. The town clerk of Liverpool wrote to thank the Lorne Scots for their help during the ordeal.[18]

We may summarize very briefly here the later stages of the long German air assault on Britain. We spoke of the 'lull' beginning in May 1941. All words are relative, and here 'lull' is one of them. It meant that for a good many months the siren was seldom heard in London; but it did not mean that the bombing of Britain stopped. In December 1940, 3793 civilians had been killed in the United Kingdom; in May 1942 the number was 399, and in July, 411.[19] When London began to hear the warnings again in 1943, the raids were on a small scale, though there was some nasty damage. In December of that year only ten British civilians lost their lives in raids, an almost unbelievably small number. February 1944 brought the 'little Blitz' on London, raising the national death-toll that month to 961. During the next few months, while the Allies were preparing for the invasion of Normandy, air activity against Britain was moderate; but there were rumours (and, in informed circles, more than rumours) of coming attacks by 'secret weapons' – pilotless aircraft and/or rockets. A few days after the Normandy landings on 6 June, the first flying bombs (v-1s) came down in England, and for the next few weeks London again was in the front line. Once more the tube stations filled with shelterers. Fatal civilian casualties for June rose to 1935. When First Canadian Army's advance up the French coast cleared the flying-bomb bases, the long-range rocket (v-2) came into action (8 September). It was more lethal than the flying bomb, but luckily much less numerous. Only 716 civilians were killed in Britain in October. As late as March 1945 the Third Reich, though now in its death throes, continued to strike at Britain with v-1s launched from aircraft, v-2s, and air bombing; 792 people were killed that month. But in April there were no casualties, and the blackout came to an unlamented end.[20]

The 60,585 civilians the Germans had killed in Britain were far fewer than the people the British and Americans (and Canadians) had killed in Germany. (A German official estimate is 593,000 dead.) And the Canadian Army's casualties by enemy action in the United Kingdom were small by comparison – 420 all ranks, of which 120 were fatal.[21]

Canada had belatedly made a special contribution to fighting the Blitz: the Corps of Canadian Fire Fighters, 411 strong.

This force had its origin in reports of devastating fire raids on British cities, and an urgent Canadian desire to help in the battle against them. The idea was actively discussed during 1940; but the Cabinet War Committee did not approve it until July 1941, and the Department of National War Services, to which the task of organization was entrusted, achieved no better speed. The corps was composed of volunteers from Canadian fire departments. Its first group did not reach Britain until June 1942, when the worst of the fire raids were long over, so it was a little like the fire brigade arriving after the fire was out. The corps was divided into four contingents, stationed in southern ports that were probable German targets: Plymouth, Portsmouth, Southampton, and Bristol. All these were raided while the Canadians were on duty there, the heaviest sufferer perhaps being Plymouth, where they fought twenty fires caused by the enemy. Portsmouth was attacked in force on 15 and 16 August 1943. The Canadian firemen did well when opportunity offered, but most of their time was spent in waiting and training. In the course of 1944 it appeared that they were no longer needed, and they returned to Canada.

Three men of the corps lost their lives in the service, only one by enemy action. Like their compatriots in the military services, some of them found wives in Britain; there were twenty-seven marriages.[22]

The Blitz, we have said, did much to break down barriers between the Canadians and their British hosts (and it is probably true that it united the British people themselves as they had never been united before). But there was a great deal of ground to make up. The problem was emphasized by a cable which General McNaughton received from the minister of national defence on 2 October 1940. It reported that Prime Minister Mackenzie King had received 'some private letters commenting on unsatisfactory discipline particularly in London and even mentioning that troops refused admission certain beverage places' (this being presumably Kingese for public houses). Five days later McNaughton replied to Colonel Ralston, saying he had discussed the situation in London with Major-General P.J. Montague, senior officer at CMHQ, and the deputy provost marshal there. 'Behaviour our men,' he wrote, 'is neither better nor worse than British.' He had no information of troops being refused admission 'to any beverage place London.' In the 7th Corps area certain establishments had been placed out of bounds to other ranks 'to meet request proprietors that their usual civilian customers be not crowded out.'[23]

Nevertheless, McNaughton found the situation far from satisfactory. It was presumably this high-level inquiry from Ottawa that led him on 15 October to send a strong letter to Canadian units and formations of the 7th Corps. It began: 'The many complaints that are reaching me regarding drunkenness and disorderly behaviour, damage to private property, slovenliness in dress, misuse of mechanical transport, dangerous driving and loss of equipment, and the indications amounting almost to a certainty that there is a considerable traffic in petrol and, to a lesser extent, in blankets and other public property are evidence of a grave failure in the discharge of their duties on the part of officers, warrant officers and N.C.O.S.' After going into some detail on these matters, the general concluded by saying that commanding officers who tackled these problems would have his full support; but 'officers of whatever rank who prove that they are unsuitable to the discharge of the high trust reposed in them will be required to give way to better men.'[24] The process of weeding out officers unequal to their responsibilities had in fact begun long since. The tougher policy announced in this letter undoubtedly had its due effect, particularly in reducing petty crime; but the gradual improvement in the situation probably owed quite as much to the Canadian soldiers' own adjustment to a new way of life and a new society.

Gradual it was. Even in the midst of the Blitz there were complaints of Canadians misbehaving. Croydon, a South London suburb where Canadian soldiers from the areas of Surrey to the west sought recreation, found the combination of bombs and transatlantic disorder hard to take. In October 1940 the chief constable of Croydon complained; drunkenness and rowdiness were the main troubles, but he also mentioned 'Canadian soldiers interfering with property left exposed by the smashing of windows consequent on the raids,' which looks like a euphemism for looting. No 6 Canadian Provost Company, stationed in London, said it was difficult for it to cover Croydon in addition to the problems it had in central London, and suggested that the units involved send nightly piquets to keep their men in Croydon in order.[25]

Relations with the people of Croydon improved over the winter. As Christmas approached, officers of the 2nd Field Regiment RCA, stationed at nearby Addington, asked the local

The Kennard's department store in Croydon entertains the
2nd Field Regiment, Royal Canadian Artillery, to Christmas dinner, 1940. (PAC, C 129384)

Women's Voluntary Services for help in finding a suitable place for the regimental Christmas party. The wvs went to R.A. Driscoll, managing director of Kennard's, a large department store in Croydon, with the result that the party for 500 men was held in the store's restaurant. The Red Cross supplied 700 pounds of turkey, and the staff of Kennard's donated beer and cigarettes. Mr Driscoll and twenty-four members of the staff waited on the men. At the climax of the meal the lights were turned out, a pipe organ played, and Santa Claus (Mr Driscoll) led in a procession of choirboys singing a carol; the leading boys carried a sign reading 'Kennards say Welcome to our Canadian Cousins.' 'A welcome and Xmas wishes were extended by Santa Claus, followed by the presentation of amusing gifts to various members of the Regiment ... At each man's place there was a handkerchief, the gift of Kennard's, accompanied by a note from one of the lady clerks.' It's not surprising that the regiment presented Kennard's with an inscribed silver tray to show their appreciation.[26]

In the areas where Canadians were billeted things were getting much better. In the village of Bletchingly, in Surrey, east of Reigate, the 1st Canadian Divisional Signals moved into winter quarters on 23 September 1940 and at once began to make themselves agreeable to the people. Even little Bletchingly had had its bombs. On the 26th the unit helped move furniture out of the bombed area, earning a letter of thanks from the local Women's Voluntary Services. By Christmas, relations were so close that on 21 December the Signals put on a party for the children of the village, the cost being met partly by voluntary contributions from the men in Regimental HQ and No 1 Company, while the rest came from the officers. In the

Santa Claus, a sergeant major in the Canadian Army, gives presents to evacuee children in Farnham on 22 December 1941. (DHist, DND, 5348)

morning 165 children under ten were entertained, in the afternoon 200 over ten came. 'A short programme was arranged and "Mickey Mouse" pictures shown and afterwards Santa Claus, as personified by Cpl F. Wilson, "D" Section, appeared and presented all with a small gift.' The people of Bletchingly reciprocated. On the 23rd the ladies of the village put on a party for the troops at the village hall, ending with dancing. 'The adjutant and oc "K" Sec. both made the finals of the dancing marathon,' but it was won by a British colleague, a signalman from 12th Div Sigs. On Christmas Day 'Many men enjoyed the hospitality of the villagers,' the people 'going to a great deal of trouble to see that everyone spent an enjoyable Christmas.'[27] The 1st Divisional Signals was one of the pioneers[28] in an activity that became a Canadian tradition. In subsequent years Christmas parties for English children became almost universal among Canadian units. Much candy and gum from parcels from Canada found its way to the small guests on these occasions, as did toys – boats, rag dolls, aeroplanes – made by the hosts.

It is an interesting point that the Canadians – particularly in the difficult early days – got on rather better with the Scots than with the English. Every witness affirms this distinction. It takes time to get to know the English; but the old legend that there is a 'special relationship' between Canada and Scotland got much support from events following that day when the troopships carrying the first Canadians came up the Clyde. It had been a standing joke in 1914–18 that when a Canadian got a week's leave he asked for a railway warrant to Edinburgh, Glasgow, or perhaps even Inverness. The same thing

A corporal in a French-speaking company of the Canadian Forestry Corps shares his chocolate bars with two young Scottish friends. His ribbons of the first war include that of the Military Medal. (DHist, DND, 19701)

happened now. Part of it, perhaps, was an inherited (and possibly Scottish) desire to get as much out of the army as you could: Why ask for a short free trip when you could get a long one? More important, however, was the fact that in Scotland Canadians tended to feel at home. A censorship report for the period 8–21 December 1941 quotes a soldier from a 3rd Division Reinforcement Unit as writing, 'The English are quite friendly, but the Scotch are more so'; there are several other letters from the same unit to the same effect. These writers had presumably been in England only a short time, but earlier arrivals would have told the same story.

Some Canadians were stationed in Scotland. The first men of the Canadian Forestry Corps (which was recruited mainly from bush workers) arrived there late in 1940, and by 1942 thirty companies (about 7000 officers and men) were cutting in the Scottish forests, producing timber which otherwise would have had to be imported in ships which were desperately scarce; it was estimated that one company produced timber roughly equivalent to that carried by a ship of 6000 tons 'plying regularly from Canada under war-time conditions.' After the invasion of Europe ten Canadian forestry companies were employed on the Continent.[29] Undoubtedly the presence of the Canadian foresters was partly responsible for the fact that 6141 Scottish women married Canadians during the war. In addition, 524 married Newfoundlanders; which reminds us that a civilian Newfoundland Overseas Forestry Unit also served in Scotland.[30] Of course, not all the Newfoundland bridegrooms were foresters; many men from the island served in the British armed forces.

One group of Canadians were certain to have special problems in adapting to life in England: those whose mother tongue was French. There were great numbers of them, though no one can say precisely how many; people enlisting were not required to state their racial origin or mother tongue. Some were in specifically French-speaking units – the Canadian Army Overseas had four infantry battalions *de langue française*, in addition to a good many units of other arms – while many were in units that were predominantly English-speaking. A large number of them spoke English, but many had only French (the census of 1931 indicates that nearly 1,800,000 Canadians spoke no other language).[31] As we have seen the young serviceman from Canada often had trouble adapting to English ways even if his language was English; how much more difficult was the problem of the unilingual French Canadian! It finds particularly poignant expression in a letter copied by the censor (who obviously translated it) in July 1942.* The writer is a soldier of the 3rd Engineer Battalion, which had been in England only a few weeks: 'I am very unhappy. I am on seven days leave in London and it is very dreary as you know that I do not speak any English. I assure you that it is not funny. I have

---

*In September 1941 the British field censors, who read Canadian as well as British army mail, began to render fortnightly reports on the letters they had examined. These reports were a valuable index of the state of the troops' morale, and are of great interest to the historian. Of course, the letters examined were not interfered with unless they contained breaches of security; they were simply resealed and dispatched to their destinations. Some civilian as well as military mail was commented on or quoted. The names of writers were never given.

Men of the Royal Montreal Regiment help an English farmer's
daughter bring in the hay in September 1942. (DHist, DND, 912-6)

been in London for three days and I have not spoken a word of French. I do not know whether I shall ever be able to speak English but I am very unhappy ... You can see how homesick I am this evening. I am alone in my room and I have been crying like a child.'[32]

Obviously, if a French-speaking soldier was to be at all at home in England he had to acquire some knowledge of the local language. Undoubtedly he frequently contrived this on his own. But the army gave official help; a part of its education program was providing facilities for French-Canadian soldiers who wished to learn English, and many took advantage of them.[33]

It would be a mistake, however, to think of the French-Canadian soldier generally as spending his time merely longing for home. The 4th Medium Regiment, Royal Canadian Artillery, landed in England on 19 August 1942 and went into billets at Bookham, Surrey. It was one of the French units that chose to keep their war diaries in English. On 21 August the diarist recorded, 'The civilian population of Bookham is taking a great interest in us. Already two invitations are received; young officers are requested. All our soldiers are being received everywhere also; most of them have already made many girlfriends [surely exceptionally fast work!]. They know that many units from Canada were located in this vicinity before us, and had the same girlfriends, but they do not care about it, as long as they have the girls.'

The winter of 1941–2, which followed the move of the Canadian Corps into Sussex, was probably the period when Canadian morale generally was at its lowest point. Sussex, with its magnificent Downs overlooking the sea, is a delightful county, but this was another very cold winter; the *Daily Telegraph* of 4 March 1942 said, 'It can now be stated that the first three weeks of February this year were the coldest since 1895.' Moreover, with the German Army deeply involved in Russia, Britain no longer seemed to be threatened with invasion and the Canadians seemed to have no prospect of action. The 1st Division had now been in England for two years. One of its infantry units was French-speaking, the Royal 22e Régiment, the 'Vandoos.' In Sussex that winter it got mixed reviews from the inhabitants. The field censors' report for the period 24 November–7 December 1941 quotes two comically different letters that both clearly refer to the Royal 22e. One civilian writing from Arundel says, 'I must tell you that it is like being in hell over here for one can't move in Arundel for French Canadians, and I can't bear them.' However, a lady in Littlehampton wrote: 'We have now got Canadians quite the most charming creatures I have met in this war, and as for the French ones among them words fail me to describe their delightfulness. We had been led to expect that a French Canadian and an Apache Indian were synonymous terms, but how far from the truth, and as we have experienced the London Irish and the Welsh, we are good judges of savages.' Since Arundel and Littlehampton are only some four miles apart, and these two letters must have been written almost simultaneously, we have here a warning to the historian against relying too implicitly upon the evidence of individuals.

Of the two local views of the Royal 22e, the adverse one seems to have triumphed. At any rate, on 23 June 1942 the

PROGRAMME OF MUSIC

TO BE PLAYED BY THE BAND OF THE

WEST NOVA SCOTIA REGIMENT,

ON BROCKHAM GREEN,

On SUNDAY, 25th AUGUST, 1940.

(By the kind permission of Lt.-Col. Gregg, V.C., M.C.),

Bandmaster: Corpl. Rhodenhiser

1. Canadian National Anthem - "O, Canada"
2. March Fantasia - - "Col. Bogey on Parade"
3. Selection - - Grand Military Tattoo
4. Overture - - - - "Beauties of Erin"
5. Cornet Solo - - - "Commodore Polka"
   Played by Sgt. Sleaunwhite
6. Waltz - - - - "Danube Waves"
7. March - - - - "To the Front"
8. Cornet Solo - - - -"Columbia"
   Played by Corpl. Rhodenhiser
9. Selection - - "Chimes of Normandie"
10. Descriptive Overture - - "Fall of Jericho"
11. March - - - - "Holyrood"
12.   "GOD SAVE THE KING"

A Collection will be made to purchase a modern Anæsthetic apparatus for the Dorking and District Hospital

The Dorking and District Hospital, Surrey, profited by this band concert given by the West Nova Scotia Regiment in August 1940.

(PAC, RG 24, vol. 15,285)

chief constable of West Sussex complained about them to Headquarters South Eastern Command. Three days later General Montgomery wrote General Crerar a 'My dear Harry' letter in his large schoolboy hand, enclosing the chief constable's report and saying, 'Perhaps you could move the battalion to another area.' And moved it was, to its surprise and regret.[34]

So far we have been talking chiefly about the army. It is time to say something in detail about the second-largest component of the Canadian military community in Britain, the Royal Canadian Air Force.*

Speaking generally, the reaction of Canadian airmen to life in Britain was similar to that of the soldiers. The differences were largely due to the operation of the British Commonwealth Air Training Plan (the RAF tended to call it the Empire Air Training Scheme), which produced many of the RCAF men who came overseas. The plan trained only aircrew — that is, flying personnel. The humbler ground-crew people were found from other sources. This meant that enlistment standards for the plan, both physical and mental, had to be high. It is fair to say that the young airmen it graduated were the cream

*The Directorate of History at National Defence Headquarters in Ottawa has lately uncovered a partial file (1941–2) of censorship reports based on examination by the British Air Ministry of letters written by RCAF men in Britain.[35] Unlike the army's, the air force censors included the names of writers and addressees. We have not reproduced these in our text. We are grateful to Dr William McAndrew of the Directorate of History for essential help in this matter.

of Canadian manhood – and, incidentally, they were not unaware of it. By no means were all of them officers. Under the original BCATP agreement[36] 'a number of pilots and observers' would be selected for commissioned rank on completion of training. In practice, most of the other graduates of the plan arrived in the United Kingdom as sergeants.

As we have already seen, the agreement provided that the Canadian airmen sent overseas should be 'placed at the disposal' of the British government. They were, however, paid at Canadian rates, Canada in the beginning paying only the difference between the British and Canadian rates. And, as with the army, the fact that the Canadians were better paid was a source of friction between British and Canadian airmen. As a result of these arrangements, the RCAF men in Britain were under the authority of the Royal Air Force. Their situation was quite different from that of the Army. Even when a Canadian Army formation was placed under higher British command, a Canadian soldier normally saw little of British military authority, unless he had a run-in with the military police; he was under a Canadian sergeant, a Canadian colonel, a Canadian general. But an RCAF sergeant might find himself under an RAF warrant officer, whom he not infrequently disliked. In the early days the situation was embittered by the fact that many sergeants who had hoped to be pilots – everybody wanted to be a pilot – found themselves instead WAGs (wireless operator/air gunners). The situation was not improved by the further fact that Canadian training in the first days of the Air Training Plan was clearly inferior to that in British establishments – Canadian letters frequently admit this – and Canadians found

At a New Year's party given by No 1 Canadian Army Service Corps Reinforcement Unit, Farnborough, Hampshire, 31 December 1942. (DHist, DND, 1023-29)

Two soldiers at the Canadian Records Office, Acton, London, confer
on the next stage of toy-making for English children, November 1943. (DHist, DND, 26242)

The Canadian Bomber Group gives a party for the children of an orphans' home in Hull, November 1943. At right, Air Commodore (later Air Vice-Marshal) C.M. McEwen. (RCAF, PL 22899)

Nursing sisters of No 14 Canadian General Hospital, Farnham, Surrey, distribute apples to evacuee children, Christmas, 1941. (DHist, DND, 5345)

themselves repeating in England courses they had been through in Canada.

The Air Ministry censors, like those in the British Army, were clearly somewhat appalled by what they read in Canadian letters in 1940–1. In a report on 'R.C.A.F. Personnel in Britain,' undated but based on letters written in February to April 1941,[37] they noted that 'shortly after Christmas' they had suggested that a large number of Canadians in Britain were unhappy. 'The damp, to which they were unaccustomed, made them miserable; inactivity and a feeling of being unwanted lowered the morale of many and made them disconsolate and homesick. They did not understand the English, and the English did not always understand them.' This report had suggested that the mood of depression would pass in the spring. The new report stated that this, unfortunately, had not happened, at least among those who had spent the winter in Britain. 'The recent trend in this correspondence has not been towards greater enthusiasm, but rather towards greater discontent, and there is more than a suggestion of an active and growing dislike of the Englishman, though seldom of the Scot.'

The censors concluded that both the Canadian and the Englishman were partly to blame. 'The Canadian does not appear to be adapting himself at all willingly to wartime conditions and restrictions; he grumbles repeatedly about the food; and he does not readily submit to discipline. Yet on the other hand his suggestion that the Englishman cold-shoulders him may not be without foundation.' Fortunately, there was 'a brighter aspect.' 'Not all Canadians appear discontented from their letters, and not all show antagonism to the English. Their enthusiasm for combat, and their faith in their ability to overcome the enemy remain – and undoubtedly will always remain – unshaken. Their admiration for the civilian population of this country [for its courage under the bombs] is still unstintingly given.' Moreover, the 'new batch of R.C.A.F. personnel recently arrived in this country' showed a 'most infectious' spirit. 'There is certainly no lack of vigour, determination or enthusiasm here.'

Some of the bitterest Canadian complaints came from the radio school at Cranwell, and there were a number of references to a warrant officer there who made himself notorious by his use of the word 'colonial.' One letter, less literate than most, both complains and admits that Canadian behaviour has not always been all it might have been: 'We're not liked here makes us wonder why the hell we ever came ... our w.o. here gave us a lecture first morn called us a bunch of rotten Colonials in way we acted we were sure burnt up as we can't help how those ahead of us act[ed], although some of our gang make one ashamed of the name Canada, but one hated to take dirt of a bunch of conscripts who as far as we can see sure haven't any desire to be in uniform, however if it keeps up we're going to see what can be done about it, but guess all the English aren't alike, big trouble is because we have more money.'[38] An airman with a French name, writing to Montreal, wrote, 'I do not like the English officers. They have no manners and no notion of hospitality, nor do they appreciate the fact that we have left good jobs, comfortable homes, our families and wives, "a land of plenty" and our liberty to come to

One Canadian wrote that it was 'like a breath from Heaven'
to be received in a friendly English household. (RCAF, PL 10825)

English children associate themselves closely with Canadian soldiers
in examining a 3-inch mortar, August 1943. (Laurie A. Audrain, PAC / DND, PA 154977)

An English doctor and his wife entertain two Canadian airmen and
two soldiers, all from Peace River, Alberta, in November 1942. (DHist, DND, 10713)

their aid.' He too reports the warrant officer's rude remark about colonials; but he also says, 'All things considered, up to date, we have nothing about which to reproach the English government. It seems to have given orders that we should receive special attention from the N.C.O.'s, who treat us "as little gods."'[39]

Several former Canadian airmen report the hostile behaviour of RAF warrant officers, and they have an explanation for it. These men were old regulars who had slowly and painfully worked their way up through the ranks to non-commissioned and warrant rank. Now they saw and resented (in Murray Peden's phrase) 'apple-cheeked youngsters with wings who had been made sergeants after little more than a year in the service. They had to grind their teeth and salute those of us who had been commissioned, of course, but some of them gloried in the opportunity to get their own back with our Sergeants or Flight Sergeants.' In due time, however, as aircrew casualties mounted, they would realize that 'one hell of a price of admission ... went with that early promotion.'[40]

The Canadians had evidently expected to be made much of by the English, and were disappointed when this did not happen. A sergeant wrote from RAF station Finningley, near Doncaster, 'I've been in England for eight weeks now, and as yet I've never been inside the door of an English house. I've been in hotels and stores, but never has anyone even asked me up for tea. They don't know what hospitality means.'[41] Another sergeant wrote from the bomber station at Abingdon, 'People over here are not the friendly type, and also I suppose it is impossible for them to ask anyone to their house on account of rations. But they will not give one a lift in their cars. Oh! well! c'est la guerre.'[42] Yet other letters tell a different story. One man wrote (postmark Chester), 'Just to show you how nice the people here are ... Last night coming back from Chester, a woman in one of those ... racers stopped and offered me a lift ... She offered me an invitation to come to her summer place in North Wales any time at all ... We constantly get invitations like that.' He went on to speak of Lady Frances Ryder's scheme of hospitality (below, page 98), which another writer called 'wonderful': 'It is really marvellous how the people are putting themselves out to be nice to us, and the best part of it is that they seem to be enjoying it themselves.'[43] Different individuals had different experiences. But the censors' generalized statements leave little doubt that in 1941 the complainers were in the majority.

Like the soldiers, the airmen reported that they were more warmly received in Scotland than in England. One wrote from Galashiels, 'I don't like the climate in Edinburgh or the lack of heat in the hotels or houses, but I surely do like the Scotch hospitality. I don't know if it is on account of the uniform and the "Canada" [badge] but I have never known such people for friendliness and that goes for bus conductors and civilians and in fact every person with whom I came in contact.'[44] A writer from Elgin, after describing troubles in England, said, 'The people in Scotland are different altogether. They don't like the English either and think the Canadian boys are the tops.'[45]

One particular matter is worth mentioning: contacts with the Royal Family. The censors devoted a special 'supplement' to this subject, quoting twenty-four letters from airmen who

Massed pipe bands of Canadian Highland regiments marching through Hyde Park
give a lift to London's 'Warship Week' savings drive, March 1942. (DHist, DND, 643-12)

Canadian soldiers lending a hand on an English farm, June 1942. (C.E. Nye, PAC / DND, PA 147108)

The caption supplied with this photograph indicated that the two sergeants were fondling
'a couple of tasty gifts by English farm folk.' It would appear, however, that the chickens may have been
the victims of a rather dull bayonet. (DHist, DND, 135195)

'You'll see a few changes, Sir, since them Canadians moved in.'

(*Punch*, 17 Nov. 1941, reproduced by permission of the proprietors)

had had the good fortune to meet members of the family.[46] Most of them were from men who had been taken on tours of Windsor Castle and to their astonishment found themselves having tea with the queen and the princesses, and sometimes the king. They are especially notable for their expressions of admiration for the queen. The young Canadians exhausted their limited supply of adjectives in seeking to describe her. 'Gosh she's grand!' 'She is the most beautiful blue-eyed woman I have ever seen.' 'She really is stunning.' 'I would say she has personality plus.' And finally, 'The Queen is one of the most charming people I have ever met (probably because she's Scottish not English).'

It seems evident that as more and more Canadians moved on from schools like Cranwell to RAF squadrons, morale improved, though there were still complaints. Life in a squadron could be more comfortable, though very much more dangerous. Murray Peden has pointed out, however, that it was only the prewar stations that were comfortable; those built in wartime were mostly mud. A Canadian soldier who found himself attached to No 400 (formerly No 110) Squadron RCAF at Odiham, an old station, wrote, 'They should be sent to the Army for a few months or a year and they might realise how comfortably off they are. They have warm rooms, fireplaces in each room, linoleum on the floor, beds and mattresses, canteens and about five meals a day yet they think the world is against them and they are badly abused.'[47] The soldier probably didn't realize that 400 Squadron had special grievances, as one of three all-Canadian squadrons sent to Britain in 1940. The censors remarked, 'It appears that No 400 Squadron has recently been taken over to a large extent by the R.A.F.,

An Englishwoman walks her dog past Canadian signallers
using an antique Lucas lamp, April 1941. (DHist, DND, 135221)

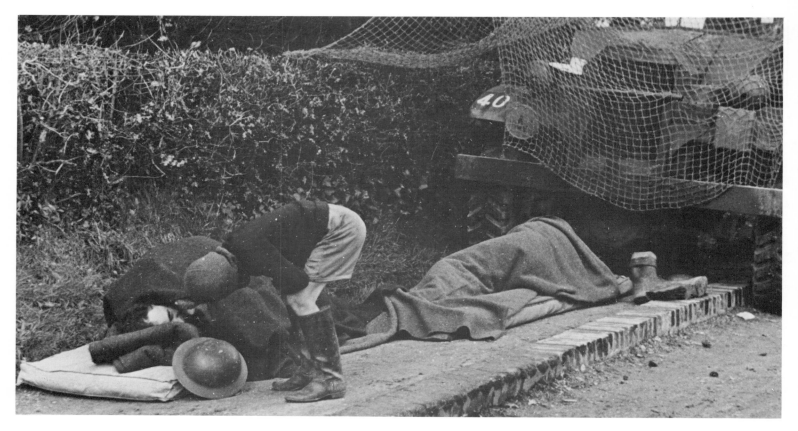

A curious English schoolboy is interested in Canadian soldiers
attempting to get some sleep after an all-night move on an exercise, April 1941. (DHist, DND, 135236)

English children seem fascinated by Canadian infantrymen
waging mimic war during an exercise in April 1941. (DHist, DND, 135223)

An airman on an RCAF bomber station in England helps on 'the extensive farm operated by the station.' (RCAF, PL 19170)

and that this has caused considerable resentment.' Instead of having their own mess, the squadron now ate with the RAF and hated it. Their letters indeed reflect violent dissatisfaction.[48]

In spite of all this, parts of the Canadian correspondence suggest the possibility that the passage of time would bring better co-operation with the RAF and a happier relationship with the English community generally. A sergeant, evidently anxious to encourage his family in Canada, writes from 'Markham' (presumably Marham, a Bomber Command station in Norfolk), 'As far as I am concerned don't worry because I just have a feeling that everything will be O.K. and rest assured that it is an honour and privilege to fight with these lads over here. I may have told you about my crew in my last letter but they are the salt of the earth and we are like a family – six guys [each] dependent on the other and each a link in this chain that will by God's grace strangle those d--- inhuman beasts that we are determined to conquer.'[49] This abuse of the enemy strikes an unusual note in this correspondence, but the account of the crew rings true. The writer doesn't tell us what its makeup was, but bomber crews were frequently very mixed and nevertheless very happy; Murray Peden's in 214 Squadron RAF included Canadians, Englishmen, and an Australian.[50]

Finally, some words from a Canadian sergeant's letter remind us how grim was the business in which these youngsters were engaged. He writes from the village of Wyton, near Huntingdon, the site of another bomber station. One of his friends, he says – this may be a letter of condolence to his family – is being buried in Wyton; and 'I can't help feeling glad that he will be in England, he loved the country so much.'[51]

A Bren gunner of the Essex Scottish gets some guidance during
an exercise in Sussex, February 1942. (O.C. Hutton, PAC / DND, PA 154972)

The smallest element of the half-million Canadians in Britain was the navy. Some Canadian sailors' opinions of Britain and the British find expression in a small number of surviving censorship reports on their letters, all of 1943–4. Not surprisingly, they are mixed. A rating in HMS *Scorpion* says Royal Navy ships 'don't feed you enough' and 'our rate of pay being higher ... causes hard feeling, and these Englishmen are not the easiest people to get along with.' He looks forward to getting back to HMCS *Niobe* at Greenock: 'It's nice there and the Scots people treat Canadians pretty good.' There's also a complaint of insufficient food from the cruiser *Belfast*. In contrast, a man in HMS *Kent* says, 'The men and Officers are grand. They sure treat me real nice.' And a rating in the battleship *Revenge* (probably serving now as a school) is full of praise for the officers: 'They are as helpful as can be towards us ... Lt. Commanders and Commanders ask us about Canada and are interested in all we do.' Apparently even the food in *Revenge* was good. The establishment called HMS *Ariel*, at Warrington, Lancashire, got high marks; it was 'better than any Canadian barracks we've ever been at'; in fact, it even had steam heat. Except for the reference to the Scots, the censors mention no reference to civilians. And the Canadian sailors, like the soldiers and airmen, complained about lack of mail and the pilfering of cigarettes in transit.[52]

It remains to look at one special circumstance affecting the Canadians' relations with the people they were living among: the fact that a considerable number of them had relatives living in England, Scotland, or both (there were relatives in Ireland

'What does C-A-N-A-D-A on the arm stand for?'

(*Punch*, 5 March 1941, reproduced by permission of the proprietors)

Cheers for Their Majesties: King George vi and Queen Elizabeth visit the 2nd Division,
then fairly recently arrived from Canada, in the Aldershot area in March 1941. (Private collection)

too, but fewer than would have been the case at an earlier stage in Canadian history). Of four Canadian airmen who have lately written about their British experiences in 1939–45 (Murray Peden, D.A. Fraser, Douglas Harvey, and Robert Collins), all had relatives in the United Kingdom and visited them. Younger relatives were apt to be absent serving in distant places, but Aunt Minnie, Aunt Kate, Aunt Martha, and Aunt Kitty – they are all in the airmen's books[53] – welcomed the Canadian relatives with open arms, treated them royally, fed them as handsomely as wartime conditions allowed, and showed them off proudly to friends and neighbours. Such connections and attentions had their due effect. The young men who had them could not feel that Britain was a foreign or an unfriendly place. The Americans who came to the country later got more official consideration, but few of them had personal ties to it. It made a difference.

CHAPTER THREE

Comrades in Arms

CANADIAN SERVICEMEN from the beginning got on better with their civilian hosts than with their 'opposite numbers' in the British services. It is true that there were plenty of difficulties with civilians in the early days, but there was steady improvement and, in the end, things really could not have been much better. Relations with Britons in uniform also grew more friendly as time passed, but there was always a degree of tension between Canadian and British servicemen. The reasons are worth examining.

It is not surprising that there should have been such troubles. If Kipling is to be believed, there were internal fights in the British regular army in his day, particularly between units from different parts of the islands:

There was a row in Silver Street that's near to Dublin Quay,
Between an Irish regiment an' English cavalree ...

That row ended in tragedy when someone drew his 'side-arm':

'T was Hogan took the point an' dropped; we saw the red blood run:
An' so we all was murderers that started out in fun.

It is not surprising either that men systematically trained to use the most extreme forms of violence against their countries' enemies should occasionally use violence against those who ought to have been their friends. Nor can the influence of *esprit de corps* be forgotten. When soldiers are told as a matter of policy that their regiment is in all respects Number One and must always be so, clashes with members of other regiments that have been told exactly the same thing about themselves are not wholly unnatural.

There were special causes of tension between the British and the Canadians. Notably, there was the fact that Canadians were better paid. In 1939 the basic pay of a Canadian private was $1.30 a day (approximately, five shillings and sixpence); that of a British private began at two shillings (roughly 50 cents) and rose with length of service and proficiency to four shillings. Taking into account the Canadian device of 'deferred pay,' by which half of the pay of men with no dependants was held back to accumulate interest for them until the end of the war, the difference was not enormous; but it was there, and the British servicemen resented it. A censorship report of March 1941 quoted a Canadian soldier's letter that tells a good deal: 'you see we make about .50 cents a day more than they do, and naturally we sort of muscle in on their girls, dames, football games and everything else going, so we have some pretty hot times, and don't think they cannot scrap.'[1] Sexual competition was certainly a major element in the situation. The general position was crudely summed up in January 1942 in a report on the morale of the 1st Canadian Division that was signed, though certainly not written, by the divisional commander, General Pearkes. It tells quite as much about Canadian prejudices as about English opinions:

Relations with the A.T.S., other Services and Allied Forces: Relations between the Div and the Home Guard are very good, with the A.T.S. [the Auxiliary Territorial Service, the British equivalent of the Canadian Women's Army Corps] intimate, but not so good with the English Army. The men of the Div are inclined to consider, with some justification, that the English tps are inferior to them in intelligence, physique, training and discipline. This strained relationship had been brought about by the unsatisfactory way in which the billets and quarters now occupied were left by the Div previously in the area; dispositions handed over to all units which had to be so radically changed; the casual and sloppy appearance of English tps on the streets and their obvious lack of discipline. One seldom sees

Canadian and English soldiers fraternizing in the public houses and places of amusement. Usually they keep in parties of either Canadian or English soldiers as the case may be. English soldiers appear to be jealous of our Canadian soldiers, who on account of their better education, intelligence and more life, appeal to the female element of society more readily than the slower witted English. I can hardly say that English offrs, N.C.O.s or men are popular with the Canadians. These remarks do not apply to Scottish units with whom relations are of the best.[2]

Obviously, one could comment at some length on this. The 1st Division, once itself so notoriously undisciplined, was now commenting adversely on British discipline. The use of the word 'intimate' in connection with the ATS was perhaps unfortunate, but quite probably deliberate. The reference to supposedly 'slow-witted' British soldiers does not sound strange to anyone who remembers Canadian conversations in England in those days, but it may prompt the reader to ask whether perhaps there may not have been the odd slow-witted man in Canadian as well as British divisions. (If the writer had only included a reference to the supposed tendency of all Englishmen to stop work at frequent intervals to make tea, he would have given a more complete summary of the current Canadian picture of the English.) We shall see that there is some testimony against the generalization that relations with Scottish units were good. The 1st Division report does not mention the important matter of pay. But there is no doubt – the evidence includes that of the censorship reports – of the unfortunate soundness of its general proposition that relations with British servicemen were far from ideal.

Actual fighting was reported almost as soon as the first Canadians arrived in Britain. In April 1940 the commanding officer of the Toronto Scottish Regiment, Lt-Col. C.C. Thompson, was sufficiently troubled by the 'animosity' to write personally to General McNaughton reporting threats against Canadians by British servicemen, combined with offensive remarks about Canadian behaviour in England during the previous war. The Scottish were at Bulford on Salisbury Plain. Thompson also reported that the men of 110 Squadron RCAF, which had arrived in England in February, were 'having a continuous battle with the Royal Tank Corps people with some pretty bad fights.'[3] Next month there was trouble in Camberley between the Welsh Guards and the Saskatoon Light Infantry.[4] In November 1940 the Canadian Corps Military Police Report mentioned a 'small fracas' between the Scots Guards and the Seaforth Highlanders of Canada 'at the Palais de Danse, Croydon'; the manager of the place was said to have blamed the Guards.[5]

Camberley, in Surrey, well known in military circles as the home of the British Army Staff College, had more than its share of disorders. At Christmas 1941 the Canadian Provost Corps in the Bordon area recorded trouble between a battalion of the British Black Watch and No 1 Canadian Armoured Corps Reinforcement Unit at Camberley.[6] A number of other references seem to be to the same affair. In January 1942 the censors quoted letters from men of the Black Watch, one of whom reported that their battalion's adjutant, speaking to the men about trouble with a Canadian unit, warned them 'not to come back with black eyes but to let them have it.' 'The men went further than the officers expected and took bayonets with them to meet the Canadians who came in trucks, and all going to different pubs. The fight began, the bayonets were drawn and the Canadians were run out of Camberley. The fight was continued some days later, when men of both regts were drunk & fighting took place all over the town. Broken bottles were used by the Black Watch.'[7] From the Canadian side, what is probably the same series of incidents is described in a letter from a soldier of the 2nd Heavy Anti-Aircraft Regiment, RCA, speaking of an unidentified 'town near us': 'The Scotch Black Watch are stationed there and a lot of our chaps went down for the Xmas celebrations. Well, the B.W.'s went round in groups, and caught the boys in ones and twos and put the boots to them. Some were badly hurt, so the next night a good-sized bunch of our fellows went down with an equally large gang of R.C. Dragoons and really taught them a lesson. Two of the Dragoons were knifed and one died this morning ... It was a very exciting time until we heard the news about the poor fellow. The town is now out of bounds to all ranks.'[8] It sounds like Silver Street over again. However, in the absence of corroboration from unit diaries or other sources,* it is quite

*The local newspapers, including the Camberley *News*, make no reference to the rioting. This no doubt was the result of censorship, either official or, more probably perhaps, self-imposed.

A Canadian Engineer sergeant explains the mysteries of baseball equipment
to girls of Britain's Auxiliary Territorial Service (the women's service of the British Army)
in September 1941. (DHist, DND, 397-4)

probable that the report of the murder was mere hearsay. But there is no doubt that Commonwealth relations were in poor shape in the Camberley area, so far as the military were concerned. This period of low Canadian morale in the winter of 1941–2 was probably also the worst moment in the Canadian soldier's relationship with the British army.

From that time there was gradual improvement. Reports of actual street fighting are less frequent in the records, and while the Canadian soldier in England cannot be said ever to have reached the point of being as friendly with British servicemen as with British civilians, there was no longer so much active hostility. The British generally were becoming more accustomed to the presence of the Canadians and to their un-English behaviour; the Canadians on their side grew steadily more at ease with England and the English. It is interesting that in 1943 and 1944 reports from the Canadian Reinforcement Units in the Aldershot area were to the effect that men fresh from Canada were the worst troublemakers.[9] By the summer of 1943 the British censors were reporting, 'Good relations are maintained between British and Canadian troops, and there appears to be a better understanding between them after association together whilst training.'[10]

Hostility to the British service people was apparently not entirely a monopoly of male Canadians. After the Canadian Women's Army Corps appeared in England in 1942, a Canadian male soldier remarked in a letter concerning the CWAC personnel of a laundry, 'I think they are about the tuffest bunch of girls I ever seen the first thing they done was get drunk and start to clean up on the ... A.T.S. ... but the English girls are well able to look after themselves.' Again one searches the official records in vain for references to this supposed battle, but there seems little doubt that it happened.[11]

Relations with another section of the British armed forces, the Home Guard, form a quite separate story from those with the 'regulars.'

The Home Guard had come into existence (at first, under the name 'Local Defence Volunteers') in the desperate crisis of May 1940, when a German invasion seemed imminent. At first it had no uniforms, just identifying armbands, and only the most rudimentary weapons; but as time passed it acquired uniforms and equipment and became more formidable. It was made up of men over normal military age, many of them veterans of the earlier war, or those in reserved occupations – very different people from the young bloods who filled the ranks of the regular units. When the Canadian Corps moved into Sussex in the autumn of 1941 it was brought into close association with the county's Home Guard. The relationship was warm on both sides. The Home Guard, an institution 'characterized by hard work, high public spirit, and no frills,'[12] commanded the Canadians' deep respect. In the summer of 1942 Colonel E.J.W. Pike, the Home Guard zone commander for Sussex (called for publication merely 'a southern county'), wrote a letter to the London *Times* giving some account of 'an intensive fortnight's training with the Canadian Forces' which his men had lately completed. It was, he said, 'an undoubted and unqualified success,' and added, 'How large a share of this success is due to the real cooperation given by the Canadians is

A baseball team from Canadian Military Headquarters plays an American team at Wembley
Park, 3 August 1942. £1000 was raised for the British Red Cross. Many of the spectators are civilians.
CMHQ won, 5-3. (C.E. Nye, PAC / DND, PA 147110)

Soccer: action around the Canadian goal during a Canadian-American
athletic meet at Tidworth, April 1943. The United States won, 3-1. (DHist, DND, 16303)

well known to the Home Guard, and the wholehearted understanding which exists between the two Forces will have lasting effects, not only during such time as they may soldier together, but in the years of peace which lie before us.' This was the second year, Colonel Pike said, in which the Canadians had devoted a special period to working with the Home Guard, and the way the men of the guard had turned out for three weekends 'at the height of the agricultural urgency' to train with them was the best tribute to the Canadians.[13]

Next year the Sussex Home Guard gave striking evidence of their appreciation of the relationship when they subscribed nearly £700 for a presentation to the 1st Canadian Corps. The corps in turn contrived to turn this into a presentation to the Home Guard. General Crerar, the corps commander, very properly thought that the shillings generously collected by the guard should stay in Sussex to serve some good purpose there. Accordingly, it was decided that part of the fund should go to the purchase of a trophy to be known as the 'Canadian Corps Trophy,' for competition among the Home Guard units of Sussex; the income from the rest would provide annual prizes for guard units deemed most efficient. These benefits would apply not only to the Sussex Home Guard but to any 'post-war military or semi-military organization which may succeed it.' The Canadian Corps Trophy was handed over to the Lord Lieutenant of Sussex, Lord Leconfield, in a ceremony on 26 September 1943.[14] Soon afterwards the 1st Canadian Corps said goodbye to the county with which it had established such special ties of friendship and sailed off to fight in Italy.

The difficulties between Canadian and British soldiers that marred the early years in comparatively peaceful England found little echo in the theatres of war. A censorship report on Canadian letters from Italy in March 1944 says, 'The British fighting soldier is continuously singled out for a special word of praise,' and quotes a writer from the 3rd Canadian Armoured Reconnaissance Regiment (The Governor General's Horse Guards): 'None of us can say too much for the British lads who go at things in such a calm and sensible way – so practical in such a chaotic business as this is at times.'[15]

A little more than two years after the first Canadians reached Britain, another and larger friendly invasion struck the island: the Yanks were coming. Much has been written on the American impact on British society. Norman Longmate has told the story in *The GIs*. Leslie Thomas in a novel has painted a convincing picture of the confrontation, and the gradual warming of the two parties, in an area where circumstances were particularly unfavourable.[16] Here we must devote at least a few paragraphs to the Canadians' relations in Britain with their fellow North Americans.

Not surprisingly, the English tended to make much of the newly arrived Americans, and the Canadians, who had been in the country so long, were sometimes moved to caustic comment.* One soldier wrote, 'The Americans over here are receiving very good hospitality. The papers are full of them.

*David Reynolds has written, 'Convinced that "public opinion" largely determined US foreign policy, the British Government spent a huge amount of time, money and effort in welcoming and entertaining the GIs – far more than they did on less important allies such as the very numerous Canadian troops – and it was hoped that this hospitality would pay dividends when the GIs returned home.'[17]

Canadian and American soldiers together watch Canada lose a
baseball game at the Canadian-American athletic meet, April 1943. (DHist, DND, 16296)

In 1943 London had an international baseball league: four US and three
Canadian teams, and an English civilian team. Here the American Headquarters team defeats
CMHQ in the opening game at Harringay Stadium, 25 April. (DHist, DND, 16436)

M.P.' organise drives to invite them out to tea and all such things. Canadians are thus maddened [sic] for they have been here over 2½ years and nothing like that was ever done. Queer world isn't it. The typical piece in the paper is – Remember these boys are 3000 miles from home etc. etc. Wonder where we come from. The people in the Midlands and Scotland are wonderful though, and do everything for the lads.'[18]

Nothing very much had ever been done officially to promote good understanding between British and Canadian troops. In the case of the Americans, in 1943 an 'Inter-Attachment' scheme was introduced, under which small parties – about an officer and ten men – were exchanged between British and American units. The plan seems to have been a success as far as it went. (One US officer, commenting on his experiences with the British and their strange habits, concluded, 'In their way the English are all right.')[19] Such a scheme would have served a less useful purpose with the Canadians, who had experienced so many contacts with the British in the course of training. Another expedient, which might well have been used to advantage with the Canadians in the early days, was a film in which the actor Burgess Meredith discussed the English for the benefit of the GIs, explaining such matters as warm beer and five-pound notes that looked like 'old diplomas.' There was also an excellent *Short Guide to Great Britain*.[20]

It was common talk among Canadians after Pearl Harbor that the men from the dominion were to be heard saying to their English friends, 'If you think we're funny, just wait; there are funnier people coming'; and that the English subsequently admitted that the Canadians had been right. The first Americans to reach the British Isles landed in Northern Ireland late

British, Canadian, and American spectators watch the opening game of the London international baseball league, 25 April 1943. Program notes helped the Britons understand a game that was strange to them. (DHist, DND, 16431)

in January 1942; and before long the American uniform was a familiar sight in London and many other parts of Britain. A couple of years later an eminent American journalist, Charles Murphy, published an article on the Canadian Army Overseas in *Fortune* magazine. He suggested that the arrival of the Americans actually worked to bring Canadians and Englishmen closer together; whereas before they had been much aware of their own differences, now they found they had things in common that the Americans did not share. Moreover, the Canadians acted as interpreters between American and Briton – the role which orators had long been fond of attributing to Canada in the English-speaking world. Wrote Murphy, 'The British, to their consternation, discovered that while the Americans had all the peculiarities of the Canadians, only in twice the intensity, they were an entirely different brand of North Americans, with infinitely more complicated racial strains. And so for the last two years the Canadians have been trying to explain Americans to the British, and the British to the Americans whom they met in the pubs.'[21]

To generalize about Canadian relations with the Americans in Britain is not easy. The Canadians were not brought into close military relations with United States troops as they were with the British, with whom the process of training kept them in fairly constant contact. They met Americans casually, in the streets and in the pubs. The contacts were further limited (and feelings not improved) by the fact that, whereas Canadian and British service clubs were open to all Allied servicemen, American clubs refused entry to all but Americans.* A Canadian sergeant on leave in Northern Ireland wrote about an experience in Londonderry: 'I slid off looking for the canteen to get a bite to eat. However instead of getting it I got asked out, was told the club was exclusively for Americans. Dam it, they go into all our Service Clubs, and are welcome, but we can't get into theirs. Same old Yankees, take all and give nothing.'[22]

The evidence of Canadian letters read by the censor, so far as it goes, suggests that Canadian relations with the 'GIS' were not particularly important, but that in this late period of the war, in which in general Canadians were on better terms with British soldiers than they had been earlier, they were not as good as those with the British. Just before the Normandy D-Day a report based on examination of over 19,000 letters written by Canadians in the expeditionary force noted that ninety-eight writers called relations with British troops good, while only twenty-eight spoke of them as bad. Of those referring to relations with U.S. troops, thirty-five called them bad, and only fourteen said they were good.[23] In both cases the figures are so small as to suggest that there was really no serious problem. Two earlier censors' remarks are worth quoting. In the summer of 1943 it was said that while there was little comment by Canadians about the Americans, 'Most comment noted seems to be critical, and refers mostly to boastfulness and having too much money to spend.' A later fortnightly

---

*There were reasons for the American attitude. The fact is that the American clubs provided a scale of amenities above those found in British and even Canadian clubs; had they been open to everybody they would have been flooded with non-Americans.

report says, 'Comments are of a mixed character and they are few in number.'[24] Actual fights between Canadians and Americans were rare. It was a distinctly unusual occurrence when in July 1942 a 'difference of opinion' between them led to extra Provost patrols being sent to Kingston-on-Thames.[25]

Canadian observers at the time amused themselves by comparing the behaviour of Canadian soldiers in English communities with that of Americans. They were certainly quite different. It was universally remarked that the Canadians always seemed to be in motion; they were going somewhere, even if it was only to the nearest public house. The Americans, on the contrary, tended to be static: what one constantly saw were rows of men in olive drab leaning against buildings and watching the girls go by: the epitome of utter boredom. One of the authors of this book, visiting Oxford at the height of the American 'occupation,' witnessed this phenomenon at its best: a long line of GIs supporting the front of the Clarendon Hotel in Cornmarket Street, idly regarding the passing show. After the end of hostilities he was in Oxford again. The Americans had gone; but they had left their mark. Across the front of the Clarendon, a yard or so above what North Americans call the sidewalk, was a long dark smudge. It was where the American backsides had rested.

Did the difference in attitude reflect the fact that the Americans were conscripts, whereas the Canadians were a volunteer army? Doubtless in part it did; remembering them now, the lounging GIs seem the picture of a force of conscripts. But, broadly speaking, the Canadians seem to have found Britain an interesting country; the reasons are presumably to be sought in their own country's history. The Americans, with a different history, in general – undoubtedly there were many exceptions – had no such feeling. On a bright Sunday morning in London the same author was riding on top of a bus. A handsome young American officer climbed aboard and, seeing another North American, sat down beside him and, in the cheerful American way, began a conversation. His subject was England. The American said he had been in the country for two months and had had more than enough of it; he was thoroughly fed up. The Canadian quietly replied that he had been there three years. The American's jaw dropped; it was clear that the mere thought of such a dreadful experience horrified him.

Far be it from the writers of this book to say whether the people of Britain liked the Canadians better than the Americans, or vice versa. The Yankees were more numerous, and got more publicity; in both cases the publicity was mixed. But it would be a pity not to record here the most famous observation ever made in England about the Americans (its author remains anonymous). The trouble with the Yanks, it was said, was that they were 'over-paid,* over-sexed, and over here.' In spite of the obvious desire of the British authorities to prevent adverse comment, one honourable member of the House of Commons complained there of the behaviour of Americans in his constituency.[27] Similar complaints might have been made about the Canadians before the Americans arrived, though they never seem to have reached the halls of

*The British soldier 'received about a quarter of the American rate.'[26]

parliament. After the Americans' arrival, the Canadians' peccadilloes perhaps seemed more minor.

One thing about the American army tended to fascinate the English and to excite constant comment: the presence in it of so many black soldiers, and the degree of discrimination that white Americans practised against them. (The social revolution associated with the name of Martin Luther King was still in the future.) David Reynolds has shown that the Churchill government, fearful of social difficulties, asked the United States to refrain from sending black troops to Britain, but the Americans refused. There were blacks in the Canadian Army too, but not nearly so many; and – doubtless just because of that – they were able to congratulate themselves on being much better off than their American brothers. There is a letter on record from a black Canadian anti-aircraft gunner: 'Most of the negro Americans here can't seem to understand why we are not separated from the whites like they are. It is a difficult question to answer, but in short it adds up to just one thing. There is no racial prejudice in the Canadian Forces. We eat, sleep, play and fight together, and each gun-crew is a well trained fighting unit with everybody protecting the other man. It is a wonderful army, this army of ours. Only one out of every hundred and fifty coloured are servants, the rest are qualified soldiers; infantry, tank, artillery, air force, navy, and last but not least the paratroops.'[28]

There were a good many contacts in sport. One deserves special mention: the two famous football games that were played in 1944, not long before the Normandy D-Day. The affair began, characteristically enough, in a meeting in a pub. Major W. Denis Whitaker of the Royal Hamilton Light Infantry, a sometime quarterback with the Hamilton Tigers, found himself sitting beside a lieutenant in the American recreational services who turned out to have a special interest in football. What was more, he had lately received from the States complete equipment for six teams. Almost inevitably, the idea of an international match arose. Whitaker approached Lieutenant-General Kenneth Stuart, chief of staff at Canadian Military Headquarters, whom he had known at the Royal Military College. Stuart was enthusiastic, and the result was the 'Tea Bowl' game played at London's White City Stadium between the Canadian Army Mustangs and the Pirates of the Central Base Section, U.S. Army.

For the Mustangs Whitaker recruited a strong team of Canadian peacetime footballers, chiefly but not entirely from his own 2nd Canadian Division. Among them were Major J.A. Nicklin, a veteran of the Winnipeg Blue Bombers, Lieutenant Orville Burke of the Ottawa Rough Riders, and Captain George Hees from the Toronto Argonauts. Thanks to Stuart's arrangements, the team had six weeks' hard training before the contest. This paid off on the day of the game, 13 February 1944.

It was a great occasion, with a crowd of some 30,000 and music at halftime by the band of Headquarters, European Theater of Operations, U.S.A., and massed Canadian pipe bands. The first half was played under American rules, and at halftime there was no score. In the second half, under Canadian rules, the Mustangs took charge. The last quarter

The two captains, Major W.D. Whitaker (Canada) and Private First Class
Frank Dombrowski (USA) with the trophy won by Canada in the 'Tea Bowl' football game, February 1944.
(Jack H. Smith, PAC / DND, PA 150135)

was dramatic. To quote a broadcast the next day by Captain Ted (afterwards Sir Edward) Leather, the Canadian manager, 'Orville Burke, who played one of the greatest games of his career, threw a forty yard pass to Denny Whitaker who romped home in the clear for the second Canadian counter.' With the score 11-6, in the last minute of play Burke threw another pass to Nicklin, who crossed the line just as the whistle blew. The Canadians won 16-6, and Whitaker, the Canadian captain, now a brigadier-general, still has the silver teapot that served as a trophy.[29]

There was, from the Canadian point of view, a less satisfactory sequel. Whitaker's arrangement with the Americans had been that there would be only one game, a 'sudden death' affair. But General Stuart while at the game had discussed a rematch with an American general. It emerged that there was a United States infantry division (referred to for security purposes as the 'Blue' Division, but actually the 29th, commanded by Major-General Charles H. Gerhardt) which had a football team that the Americans believed, with reason as it turned out, could 'put up a very much better game' than the Central Base Section boys. (The 29th, incidentally, had been the first U.S. division to arrive in the United Kingdom, and it landed on Omaha Beach on D-Day.)[30]

The generals' arrangement turned out to be awkward for the Canadians. The Canadian team had been disbanded, Whitaker had been promoted to command his battalion, and action was comparatively imminent. However, the team as far as possible was reconstituted. Nicklin was not available; he was second-in-command of the 1st Canadian Parachute Battalion, and the commander of the British brigade in which it was serving would not release him, nor did Nicklin himself care to risk an injury that might put him out of the coming operation.* George Hees was also unavailable. The Americans, however, had the advantage of the services of at least one crack professional player, Sergeant Tommy Thompson, late of the Philadelphia Eagles.

The second game, called this time the 'Coffee Bowl,' was played at the White City on 19 March, before a crowd estimated at 50,000. Thompson was the star, and the Blues, in the words of one newspaperman, 'ran roughshod' over the Mustangs.[31] A Canadian officer wrote, 'The fine display put on by the massed Canadian pipe bands compensated to some degree for the defeat.'[32] But the Canadians lost, 18-0.

When action began the Canadians had much less contact with the Americans than with the British, but it's pleasant to record one case indicating that, just as with the British, the American fighting man commanded Canadian respect when he came up against the enemy. It comes in September 1943, and curiously enough stands cheek by jowl in a censorship report with a couple of particularly unpleasant Canadian comments on Americans in England. The examiners remarked, 'From the comparatively few comments noted the relations between U.S. and Canadian troops appear to be good on the whole.' However, a private wrote in condescending terms: 'They are a

* Nicklin was killed on 24 March 1945, while commanding his battalion in the Rhine crossing operation.

Part of the crowd that watched the first of the two Canadian-American
football games at White City Stadium, February 1944. (Jack H. Smith, PAC / DND, PA 150136)

good bunch of chaps in general and very generous with their money and cigarettes, if you flatter them a little bit and tell them they are swell guys ... they will buy you anything that money can purchase besides giving you the shirt off their back. But for all their good deeds they are not the soldiers that we Canadians are, nor do they stand up on the average with Tommy Atkins – he's a pretty hard guy to beat, even though he is the lowest paid and the poorest clothed.' A lance-sergeant in the Royal Canadian Artillery wrote contemptuously about the numerous medal ribbons which almost all Americans wore, even though they had seen no action. He went on, 'The chief factor, however, in the undeniable ill feeling towards Americans shared by both Canadian and English is that one would think to hear some of their "pseudo" N.C.O.'s. talk that the Lord God Almighty had personally thanked them for coming over to this country. Most of them make too much noise, spend too much money, drink too much, spend most of their off duty hours with whores, and create a rather bad impression generally. I hope you don't mind my speaking plainly – it's a subject on which most of us feel pretty strongly.'

The voice from the battlefield is different. During 1943 about 350 officers and men of the Canadian Army in England were sent to North Africa to gain battle experience by being attached to the Allied forces fighting there. Most of them went to the First British Army; but at least one, a sergeant in the Carleton and York Regiment, joined the Americans. He was wounded and returned to England, and there he wrote this letter: 'I want to take back all I said about the American soldiers. I spoke of the ones in London, but now I was [want] to say that I met the ones in Africa, in fact I was attached to them for a while out there and believe me they are very good soldiers and the people of the United States should be proud of their fighting troops. I was attached to the 1st United States Division for over a month and my hat is off to them for their courage and fighting ability, now I know the real American soldier and I have met some very fine boys so forgive me for what I said won't you.'[33]

One thing is amply clear, and every Canadian who was there will testify to it: the Canadians in Britain did not identify themselves with the Americans. Their wartime experience in general made them more consciously Canadian than they had been before; but their particular experience in England, as the years there passed, brought them closer to the British people and gave a new reality to the Commonwealth connection. A letter written by a Canadian soldier in Italy early in 1944 perhaps tells the story as well as it can be told: 'On the whole we get on pretty well with the Yanks for after all we talk the same language as they do. But I think, if anything we are on better terms with the Tommies. Our years in England have I suppose made us more English than we realised. There is a pub (or should I say wine shop) up behind the front which the Canadians have taken over. They call it the "Sussex Inn" and have taught the Italian waiter to say "Time Gentlemen Please." You run into things like that quite often which illustrates our "Anglicised outlook."'[34] Volumes could not say more.

CHAPTER FOUR

Keeping the Troops Happy

ON 22 AUGUST 1940 Canada's high commissioner dined with Winston Churchill at No 10 Downing Street. The occasion was a party for visiting United States officers. In the course of conversation the British prime minister expressed concern 'over the problem of keeping the troops occupied over the winter.' 'The soldiers from Canada were restless now. He said there had been 10 murders among them.' Whether he meant that the Canadians were murdering one another or murdering other people is uncertain. Mr Massey commented in his diary, 'He had of course been grossly misinformed & I shall find out the facts.'[1] Just what the actual statistics then were is difficult to establish at this date. But Churchill was not the only person worrying about keeping the troops occupied when they were not busy training. The problem concerned Canadian authorities throughout the war.

From time immemorial the chief provision made for soldiers' welfare had been the presence of regimental chaplains who perhaps did little more than preach to the troops on suitable occasions and bury them when they had the misfortune to stop a bullet. The modern padre does far more than this. In the Second World War the army's Canadian Chaplain Service, which in the previous conflict had been unified, was divided into Protestant and Roman Catholic sections; the comparatively few Jewish chaplains found a place among the Protestants. This is not the place to tell the story of Canadian chaplains, either in England or on the battlefield, where they won many decorations;[2] it is enough to note that they were active far beyond the limits of their spiritual vocation. One of them wrote, 'I have organized canteens, been in charge of broadcasts, distributed libraries, promoted shows, entertainments and dances – in fact I have done almost anything and everything to help our men and promote their welfare.'[3]

Obviously, however, the regimental padre could not bear the whole burden of welfare work of this sort. During the First World War a good deal had been done in the way of organizing comforts and entertainment for the Canadian forces; and on the outbreak of the new war in 1939 many public-spirited people and organizations offered their services for such work. Within a few weeks the government announced that four voluntary organizations – the Salvation Army, the Knights of

Columbus, the Young Men's Christian Association, and the Canadian Legion – would share the work of providing 'auxiliary services' for the forces. In the beginning they were financed by private donations, but in 1941 the government itself assumed this burden.[4] The organizations worked across Canada and wherever Canadian servicemen were found; the United Kingdom, naturally, was a most important field of endeavour, particularly as it gradually became evident that a large Canadian military force was going to sit in that country indefinitely. The organizations worked mainly through 'supervisors' who were attached to units and formations of the forces and performed in much the manner of the active padre just quoted. These supervisors were paid as army captains and had the privileges of officers, though not of course any powers of command. (Chaplains were officers, but their ranks were honorary.)

A supervisor attached to an army unit had a fairly straightforward task, though not an easy one. Others had more complicated duties, notably those who tried to serve the Canadians scattered widely through the units of the Royal Air Force. The Bomber Command area was the responsibility of the YMCA.[5] The YMCA report of operations for March 1943 had this to say about the problem: 'Our present plan is to cover the entire territory, including the small locations – where even as small a number as two Canadians reside – every five weeks. Coupled with this, we will assist our Supervisors from the Leeds Office and Stores, with a mailing service of cigarettes and Red Cross Comforts, "Canada's Weekly" and "Wings Abroad" [respectively, a magazine produced commercially in London and the RCAF overseas newspaper]. Even so, our Supervisors mutually feel that their work on the large main Stations has to suffer considerably while they are "on the road," servicing the small and isolated groups of Canadians.'[6] An individual supervisor's tasks in the field tended to be much the same, whichever of the four organizations he belonged to. However, in 1941, following a report on the problem by Colonel the Hon. R.J. Manion,* the organizations agreed that in their general operations they would specialize, the YMCA taking responsibility for sports and recreation, the Canadian Legion for concerts and entertainment, the Salvation Army for canteens and cinemas, and the Knights of Columbus for arranging hospitality and social functions.[7]

From the beginning the Canadians had full access to the amenities provided for the British forces. These included the canteens run by the NAAFI (Navy, Army and Air Force Institutes), which, however, never managed to achieve much popularity with Canadians. NAAFI tea and coffee were a byword. A Canadian soldier in the Ordnance Corps wrote in 1941, 'The N.A.A.F.I. will be the cause eventually of a Major riot they charge the highest prices for the lowest quality, and their help is rude to you, also they will only give the worst service. None of them would last 10 minutes in any canteen run by efficient Canadians.'[8] This was doubtless a bit extreme, but a low opinion of the NAAFI was certainly general.

Sport was popular both with the troops and the higher

*The former leader of the Conservative party was appointed to survey the operations of the auxiliary services and recommend improvements.

The Royal Winnipeg Rifles hockey team take on an unidentified team
at the Purley arena in South London, February 1942. (DHist, DND, 5689)

authorities. A report from the 1st Canadian Division in April 1940 made the obvious but unquestionable point that the playing of games 'eliminates to a large extent the cause of trouble in towns and villages, and contributes in large degree to an improvement in [the troops'] state of mind and physical fitness.'[9] Sports equipment was an item in constant demand from supervisors. The Hastings and Prince Edward Regiment in Aldershot recorded in January 1940 that the YMCA had provided what was needed for softball, soccer, and rugby. By March the Hasty Pees were playing soccer against a British unit of the Royal Army Service Corps and softball against the 48th Highlanders of their own brigade. Their diarist wrote, 'Soccer is an excellent game and there is growing interest, but most of the troops still congregate at the softball diamond.'[10] In October of that eventful year the RCAF Headquarters in London passed to the Auxiliary Services at Canadian Military Head-quarters (on which at that early date they still depended in such matters) an urgent request from No 1 Squadron RCAF, then resting at Prestwick after their distinguished share in the Battle of Britain (above, page 24), for equipment for softball, baseball, volley ball, boxing, and hockey: 'anything which your Services can do to keep their minds off air fighting whilst they are at rest, will be more than appreciated by this Head-quarters.'[11] Undoubtedly everything available was promptly sent off.

The preference for familiar Canadian kinds of sport is evident. Ice hockey might have been a serious problem; but luckily England was not devoid of ice rinks. The Imperial Ice Rink at Purley on the south edge of London was adjacent to the areas of Surrey where Canadian soldiers were so numerous. By October 1940 the YMCA had arranged to take it over for hockey and pleasure skating. It was to open by 1 November, but German bombs caused delay. By 11 December it was reported that 200 men were playing hockey there daily, and there were 500–600 skaters on Saturday and Sunday after-noons. The Sports Stadium rink at Brighton was also rented for the Canadians that winter.[12]

As time passed, sport became more highly organized and competition within and among the services was on a large scale. Witness the YMCA report for July 1943, which recorded the 'all-wartime peak reached by Sports events in the Army and Air Force': 'Every Unit and Squadron, Brigade and Station, Formation and Air District conducted eliminations in Track and Field, and other kinds of Sports all leading to the Army and R.C.A.F. finals. In the Army alone there were 17 formation final events which had 2,098 athletes participating and 31,500 spectators. These numbers would be many times multiplied were the preliminaries taken into account. Such activities are of inestimable value to the character and morale of the troops. The R.C.A.F. championships in Track and Field were very successfully conducted on July 24th and the Army finals will be held on August 14th.'[13] Competition in the major sports was usually between Canadian service teams or sometimes with teams from British or Allied (particularly US) forces. Occa-sionally, however, Canadians played against civilian teams, including British baseball clubs in Dagenham, Manchester, and Hornsey.[14] If you couldn't play, you could watch. Spec-tator sport in the Canadian forces in Britain probably reached

**SECOND
CANADIAN INFANTRY BRIGADE**

Brigade Commander : BRIG. G. R. PEARKES, V.C., D.S.O., M.C.

Comprised of the

**Princess Patricia's
Canadian Light Infantry**

Officer Commanding : LIEUT. COLONEL W. G. COLQUHOUN, M.C.

49th Edmonton Regiment

Officer Commanding : LIEUT.-COLONEL W. G. STILLMAN.

Seaforth Highlanders of Canada

Officer Commanding : LIEUT.-COLONEL J. B. STEVENSON

---

*The Bands of the three Regiments will provide music during the
afternoon*

List of Events

1. POLE VAULT
2. THROWING THE DISCUS
3. 880 YARDS RELAY (4 × 220)
4. TUG-OF-WAR (Heats)
5. TWO MILE RELAY (4 × 880)
6. THROWING THE JAVELIN
7. HIGH JUMP
8. 440 YARDS RELAY (4 × 110)
9. THROWING THE HAMMER
10. HOP, STEP AND JUMP
11. ONE MILE RELAY (4 × 440)
12. THREE MILES RACE
13. PUTTING THE WEIGHT
14. LONG JUMP
15. TUG-OF-WAR (Final)
16. ONE MILE TEAM RACE

All events except Tug-of-War count for regimental points

POINT SCORING : FIELD EVENTS 3, 2, 1. TRACK EVENTS 6, 4, 2

PRESENTATION OF PRIZES
BY
MRS. G. R. PEARKES

REFRESHMENTS

GOD SAVE THE KING

From the beginning, sports competition helped to maintain morale. This is the program for
the 2nd Canadian Infantry Brigade's track and field meet in May 1940. (PAC, RG 24, vol. 15,253)

its highest point in the two Canadian-American football games at White City in 1944 described in chapter 3.

The navy was not forgotten. From the beginning, when Canadian ships came into British ports, efforts were made to provide recreation for their crews. We find the commander of the destroyer *Saguenay* in October 1940 acknowledging sports equipment and games sent by the Auxiliary Services at CMHQ.[15] At a later stage, when the RCN's shore depot, HMCS *Niobe*, was set up at Greenock, it got the same help as army or air force units. In July 1943 the YMCA reported, 'Sports continue to be the highlight of our work there.'[16]

The Auxiliary Services supervisors with units, who as time passed were provided with military helpers, performed many tasks besides promoting sports. They ran movies twice weekly, singsongs, bingo games, quiz programs, amateur shows, and bridge, cribbage, and darts tournaments. They provided stationery and distributed free the cigarettes donated by firms and individuals in Canada, operated mobile canteens, and organized reading and writing rooms and libraries. The latter were stocked with educational and technical books but fiction had the greatest circulation, especially westerns and detective and short stories. The chief demand, however, was for such American magazines as *Saturday Evening Post, Collier's*, and *Liberty*.[17] In short, the supervisors did everything that circumstances permitted to keep the men agreeably occupied during their hours off duty.

Providing for men on leave was a different problem. A serviceman on leave usually made for a city, and more often than not it was London. The capital, we have already seen, continued to be a magnet for Canadians even while it was under almost constant air attack. What the man on leave needed was cheap and decent accommodation, cheap and palatable food, and agreeable entertainment. Entertainment was not hard to find; after all, providing it had always been one of London's industries, and even the Blitz at its worst did not wholly put a stop to it. The man who wanted less respectable amusement could always find it. Its purveyors, the 'Piccadilly Commandos,' were active on the streets.[18] As for the other requirements, both private and official agencies worked hard to produce them.

The Canadians arriving at the end of 1939 found a welcome at the various London hostels set up to accommodate British troops. Two of the best-known were the King George and Queen Elizabeth Victoria League Club in Malet Street and the Union Jack Club opposite Waterloo Station. Various other volunteer organizations helped the visitors. For a good many years Lady Frances Ryder had operated a much-appreciated scheme arranging private hospitality for students from the dominions studying in England. She now converted this into a plan to arrange similar invitations for dominion officers. This continued until 1941, when it was taken over by the Knights of Columbus, on an all-ranks basis. Lady Frances, however, continued her service for officers through a series of Sunday tea-dances which many Canadians enjoyed.[19] An ex-officer has recently recalled that it was at one of these dances that he met his wife.

It was not only affluent citizens who opened their houses to Canadians. Patricia Macoun, who was serving with the

Canadian airmen engaged in a typically English amusement,
darts, at an 'advanced airfield,' September 1943. (RCAF, PL 19850)

This group of singers, from No 27 Company of the Canadian Forestry Corps,
includes men from every province of Canada. (Lt T.F. Rowe, DHist, DND, 19704)

Canadian sailors and friends roller-skating at Londonderry, the port in Northern Ireland that served as a base for convoy escorts, January 1945. (F.R. Kemp, PAC / DND, PA 147132)

Women's Royal Canadian Naval Service in London, remembers that she and another Wren, seeking a weekend away from v-bombs, went to the Knights of Columbus and found themselves in the modest home of a bus driver and his wife in Epsom. Their host and hostess couldn't have been 'kinder or more welcoming.' But the bombs were in Epsom too, and the whole party spent the night under the stairs.[20]

The first Canadian establishment in London to offer hospitality to the services was apparently the B.C. Services Club at British Columbia House, which claimed to have opened 'within 48 hours of the arrival of the first Canadian [Army] contingent in England,' in December 1939. A canteen 'conducted under the auspices of the Y.M.C.A. and staffed by the voluntary services of the Canadian Women's Club' provided Canadian dishes, and there was also a recreation room.[21] The most famous Canadian hospitality centre in London, however, was the Beaver Club.

The Beaver Club was the heir of the Beaver Hut in the Strand, operated by the YMCA in the First World War. It was set up in the former London County Council building in Spring Gardens, just out of Trafalgar Square and close to Canada House. The moving spirit behind it was Vincent Massey, who was chairman of its Board of Management and devoted a great deal of time to the project. Accustomed to getting his own way, he was displeased when obstacles presented themselves in the early days. The YMCA was the organization primarily associated with the project. After a meeting on 22 January 1940 he recorded 'a most unhelpful attitude of competition from the Canadian Legion and Salvation Army people encouraged I am afraid by Brig. [W.W.] Foster [director of auxiliary services], whose function was intended to be that of co-ordination.' However, on 18 March he wrote that it was 'very hard to keep the whole soul-saving tract-pushing tendencies of the Y.M.C.A. personnel from getting out of hand. If it did it would injure the Club seriously.' On 12 April he complained about the attitudes of the 'Canadian colony' in London: 'the more you try to do the more you incur rancour and jealousy.'[22]

The club opened in February 1940 and, like many other enterprises, it acquired new life and vigour in the dramatic days after the Dunkirk crisis. On 15 July Massey wrote, 'the Club is now tremendously active – 9,000 admissions in a single week. Half the men using it are Canadians, and the others British, Australian, New Zealand and of all three services. It seems to have finally reached full usefulness and all the bickering and gossip of the place has vanished under the pressure of hard work.'

The Beaver Club offered a wide variety of services: a canteen featuring Canadian-style food, writing and reading rooms, games rooms, an Information Bureau where the serviceman could get all kinds of facts about London, including particulars of available accommodation, and assistance in planning leaves throughout the country; checking, banking facilities, showers and baths, and a barber shop. A large corps of voluntary women workers helped to staff the club. One member of the staff, Marion Walwyn, director of the Information Bureau and Programmes, had worked in the old Beaver Hut of 1914–18.[23]

From the beginning the club was enormously popular. One reason appears in a letter written by a Canadian sergeant in

Men of the Royal Regiment of Canada lining up for food and drink at a
YMCA canteen, April 1943. (Frank Royal, PAC / DND, PA 150138)

1945, probably concerning VE-Day: 'I spent the biggest part of the day in London. Had supper at the Beaver Club, and what do you think it was? Waffles with real maple syrup and coffee with cream floating on top – boy, was it ever good!'[24] Inevitably, this sort of thing attracted British servicemen, who had few such facilities of their own. Canadians began to complain that they were being crowded out of their own club. Nobody wanted to follow the American example and close the club to non-Canadians. Seeking a solution, Massey went to see General Sir Arthur Smith, commanding the London District, and found him understanding. But whatever measures Smith took, the problem persisted.[25]

The Beaver Club was financed to a large extent by private donations; Massey mentions receiving a cheque for £5000 from Garfield Weston. But the deficit (in 1941 some $50,000) was covered by the YMCA.[26]

The Beaver Club was for 'other ranks'; officers did not share in its benefits. Alice Massey, however, organized nearby (in Cockspur Street, just across from CMHQ) a more modest Canadian Officers' Club which functioned throughout the war. Run by Mrs Massey and some women volunteer helpers, it was primarily a place where one could have a simple lunch in agreeable company. On most days Mrs Massey herself was behind the table dishing out the stew: 'Take a spoon,' she used to say.[27] Many people have pleasant recollections of it. It is a surprise to find in a Roman Catholic padre's war diary a report of complaints that Canada could not produce a better club for her officers.[28] Perhaps the complainants disliked the absence of drink – Mrs Massey's club was dry, except on high days and holy days when there was punch. But in London, after all, there was no lack of licensed premises where an officer could quench his thirst. It was said that the bar of the Park Lane Hotel was like a little bit of Canada – that is, until the American invasion of it, after which the Canadians were seen there no more. Moreover, many London clubs opened their hospitable doors to Canadian officers. The East India and Sports Club in St James's Square is one that many remember with gratitude.

This may be a good place to say a word about the Masseys. Vincent Massey certainly had his failings. Beyond doubt – as his own memoirs[29] amply show – he was a snob, and he dearly loved a lord. Yet it must be said that on the whole he was a good high commissioner, who did his utmost to see that Canada's interests were not overlooked by a British government which was not normally much disposed to be aware of them;[30] and the good relations which he cultivated with important British personalities were to Canada's advantage. He undoubtedly worked tirelessly in the interest of Canadian servicemen in Britain; the Beaver Club was only the most important of his enterprises in this field. As for Alice, his wife, she had not been universally popular in Canada; some said she had been responsible for his failure to be elected to the House of Commons in 1925, and to some of the group of people active around Hart House Theatre at the University of Toronto her name was anathema. But in England during the war she found her vocation, and it was seldom one heard an unkind word

A Halifax bomber is the background for a baseball game
in the Canadian Bomber Group area, March 1944. (RCAF, PL 28521)

about her. Certainly the Canadian officers who frequented her little club – sometimes known as 'Mother Massey's Hash-House' – had nothing but good things to say about her.

The Beaver Club did not provide overnight accommodation, and hostels to do this were important to the serviceman. Some British hostels we have already mentioned, and Canadian ones soon began to appear. All four Canadian voluntary organizations opened hostels in London. On 28 May 1940 Massey was present at the opening of the Salvation Army hostel at the West Central Hotel in Southampton Row, writing in his diary, 'A rather moving occasion through the sincerity of all the Salvation Army personnel present.'[31] This was not the only time he paid special respects to the 'Sally Ann'. At Christmas of 1942 he went the round of the hostels and noted 'as always a feeling of real "heart" at the Salvation Army.'[32]

The German Blitz of 1940–1 hit the hostels as it did the rest of London, and created special problems. The damaging raid of the night of 16–17 April 1941 cost more Canadian lives than any other – twenty-five in all, two from the RCAF, one from the RCN, and the rest from the army.[33] This raid caused a serious shortage of accommodation for troops on leave in London, and the British War Office issued orders forbidding British soldiers to spend the night in London, except where there were compassionate grounds. The Canadian Corps forbade leave to London unless the man concerned was staying with friends. The soldiery, however, had no intention of allowing either the Germans or their own generals to exclude them from the capital. They were not deterred by the still worse raid of the night of 10–11 May, the heaviest London ever suffered.

Nobody knew at the time that it was also the last of the great raids; the Luftwaffe was shifting east in preparation for Hitler's attack on Russia on 22 June.

A conference at Corps Headquarters on 6 June was told that in London 'last week-end, out of 2300 beds available for all British and Empire Fighting Services,' 800 were occupied by Canadian soldiers. General McNaughton then said that as long as the corps was in its present area, men could not be prevented from going to London, and any drastic restrictions would only lead to absence without leave; accommodation must therefore be increased. Major J.M. Humphrey, senior officer of auxiliary services at CMHQ, was asked to discuss the matter with the voluntary organizations.[34] As a result, new Canadian hostels were opened. Ultimately there were eleven of them in London, including one for officers.[35]

London was the greatest problem but not the only one. Canadians on leave visited other cities throughout the United Kingdom, and here too accommodation was needed. By October 1944 there were eleven more hostels in cities in the English 'provinces,' Scotland, and Northern Ireland. In addition, the Knights of Columbus Canadian War Services operated hospitality bureaus in all the principal cities, twenty in all. These bureaus made arrangements including 'free hospitality in private homes, some free hospitality in Clubs and accommodation at a nominal charge.'[36] A Salvation Army hostel in Londonderry particularly served the crews of the naval escort vessels that worked out of that port late in the war.[37] A Canadian private wrote from Edinburgh, 'We are staying at the Canadian Legion Club and everything is very nice. A nice

A muscular female impersonator scores a hit
at a Canadian Bomber Group party, May 1943. (RCAF, PL 19056)

bedroom with warm Canadian blankets and quilts. The meals are tops.'[38] It would not be hard to compile an extensive anthology of soldiers' appreciations of the benefits received from the work of the four voluntary organizations.

'Live' entertainment – stage shows, particularly musical ones – was another great requirement, much appreciated by the troops when the quality was good. Here, too, the Canadians had access to the arrangements made for the British services. The British organization set up for the purpose was ENSA – the Entertainments National Service Association. It is sad to have to report that the Canadians in general disliked the ENSA shows; and – though some readers may find this hard to believe – they disliked them mainly because they were dirty. Everyone who was there will support this statement. An officer reports 'sitting through one of the poorest concerts I've ever seen anywhere. It was really lousy. The entertainers were awful and their jokes dirty.' The same censorship report contains another scathing comment: 'Last night we all attended the rankest foulest Ensa show yet. I think we all had nightmares last night. And to top it all they had to come to the mess afterwards.'[39] One Canadian ex-officer claims that in his unit an accepted punishment for defaulters was obliging them to attend an ENSA show. General McNaughton himself is on record on ENSA. At a conference in 1941 he said 'He was not satisfied with the type of show that ENSA was giving which, from his own personal experience, had on occasion been vulgar.'[40] Vulgar, alas, was ENSA's middle name.

The remedy was obvious: Canadian shows. There had been

good Canadian concert parties in the first war, notably the famous 'Dumbells.' Getting an entertainment organization going took time, but in the end all three Canadian services had excellent shows of their own. Ottawa, it must be said, did not always display much imagination in the matter. The minister of national defence personally intervened to get Raymond Massey, who was thinking of joining the US Marines, to come back to the Canadian Army, in which he had served in 1914–18. And Massey, one of North America's most distinguished actors, was put into the section of the adjutant-general's branch in Ottawa that dealt with matters of recreation and entertainment and set to 'pushing paper.' After a year or so during which he was never once invited to make any use of his acting talents he wangled his release, returned to the United States, and, to the disgust of his brother Vincent, became an American citizen.[41]

Canadian unit concert parties sprang into existence more or less spontaneously, and were actively encouraged. Some of them were clearly first-rate; we hear of the party from No 1 Canadian Artillery Holding Unit giving a 'splendid performance' at the Cambridge Theatre, London.[42] The first official army party was the Tin Hats, formed under Canadian Legion auspices, who began performing in September 1941 and presented their show at the Ambassadors Theatre, London, on 9 October.[43] The Masseys were present, and didn't much approve. The high commissioner wrote, 'It depressed us both & we were entirely disingenuous in offering congratulations to the company at its conclusion.'[44] Massey's standards were high. No doubt, also, the show improved with time. The people it

was meant for seem to have liked it. The censors reported in November, 'The "TIN HATS" appear to have earned approbation, and are very popular.'[45] Next month approval was given for the Tin Hats to visit RCAF stations.[46] Shortly, other army concert parties were at work: the Haversacks, the Kit Bags, the Bandoliers, and the Forage Caps. The Tin Hats went to France in July 1944. Unfortunately, the ship conveying them was involved in an 'incident' which left three of the troupe missing.[47]

The Canadian groups were given the use of London theatres on Sundays and Mondays, when they would otherwise have been dark, and the audiences were mainly Canadian service people. In due course the RCAF organized its own concert parties, most if not all of them coming from Canada. First were the Blackouts, who opened at the Comedy Theatre, London, in December 1943. Next came the All Clear, in August 1944. There were also the W-Debs (the reference is to the WD, the Women's Division of the RCAF), Swing Time, the Tarmacs, and the Air Screws.[48]

The Army Show, formally so called, was organized in Canada and did not get overseas until the end of 1943. It began as a creation of the Directorate of Recruiting, and toured Canada for some time in the interest of drumming up enlistments. It was commanded by Major W.V. George. When it arrived in England it broke up into five groups and toured English camps before following the troops to the Continent and the battlefronts. Its members were skilled performers (Johnny Wayne and Frank Shuster got their start in it) and the presence of girls of the Canadian Women's Army Corps was

An RCAF squadron celebrates Hallowe'en, 1943:
A feature of this costume party was a draw for Victory Bonds. (RCAF, PL 22341)

The brass section of the RCAF Overseas Dance Band, October 1943. This band contributed to variety shows that were shipped in recorded form to radio stations throughout the world. (RCAF, PL 22035)

The RCAF concert party 'All Clear' works the bureaucrats over, August 1944. (RCAF, PL 32189

The orchestra and cast of the first Canadian all-soldier musical revue, the Tin Hats,
in the finale of their show at London's Ambassadors Theatre, 9 October 1941. (DHist, DND, 5043)

particularly appreciated. Soldiers' letters in the late winter of 1944, a few weeks before D-Day, shouted approval. 'We had a Canadian Army show here a couple of weeks ago, there was seven girls and five men all Canadians. It sure was good. Our sense of humour is quite a lot different from the English people's and it being the first all Canadian show we have seen since we came over here it sure was appreciated.' 'We had a great Canadian show last night, five girls and five men, sure was a nice one, and it sure sounds nice to hear a Canadian voice.' 'An all Canadian stage show hit the camp the other night, eight c.w.a.c.s and numerous Army personnel. It was the best show I have seen in England, and have seen very few better in Canada.'[49] At least some of the writers may have been recent arrivals, who had not benefited by the work of the army concert parties organized overseas, but the tribute to the Canadian Army Show is striking.

It was the navy, however, that hit the jackpot. The RCN show from Canada, 'Meet the Navy,' opened at the London Hippodrome on 1 February 1945, and Vincent Massey truly said it was 'absolutely first rate': 'It was thoroughly *Canadian* — it could not have been American or English.'[50] The dancing and choreography by Alan and Blanche Lund, now at the beginning of a great career, were splendid, and the hit of the show was John Pratt singing 'You'll Get Used to It':

> You'll get used to it; you'll get used to it,
> The first year is the worst year;
> Then you'll get used to it.

The show did a limited tour in England, and later went to the Continent. One soldier wrote, 'Lady Luck was with me again this week: the Navy show from Canada was in Aldershot, and our o.c. managed to get fifty reserved seats, after having a draw I was one of the lucky. I really enjoyed it after seeing so many English shows. I don't get much kick out of them, they're really corny.' Another military critic commented, 'I was down to another camp to see the Royal Canadian Navy stage show and it was really something to see. I have seen quite a few stage shows, but nothing like that one ... I would give anything to see it again.'[51]

'Meet the Navy' was a magnificent piece of public relations, and a delight to the service men and women who could see it; but apart from the fact that it came overseas when the war was almost over, it was a large and elaborate show which could be staged only in a big, well-equipped theatre, and so comparatively few could see it. Unlike the five segments of the Army Show, it could not go out to the people in the field. Of course, the navy's entertainment problem was different from those of the other services. Concert parties could not be put on corvettes on the North Atlantic; the fighting sailor had to get his entertainment in port. It was not the navy's job to entertain the other services, but 'Meet the Navy' in fact did bring them enormous pleasure, which was duly appreciated.

News from home! It was one of the most persistent demands of the Canadian serviceman overseas, but it was not an easy one to satisfy. Paper shortage reduced the British daily newspapers to mere shadows of their peacetime selves, and the Canadian searched them in vain for information about his native country. Canadian politics, Canadian sport, Canadian everything, were missing. Canada might have been on another planet. Months-old papers and magazines from home were eagerly devoured. Once again, Canadian official action alone could fill the gap; and, as usual, the wheels moved slowly.

The answer, useful if not totally adequate, was the weekly *Canadian Press News*, which first appeared in May 1942. As the name implies, it was the result of the co-operation of the Canadian Press news agency, which provided the content and makeup from Canada. It was an austere four-page paper, containing no editorial comment or opinion, and in its early days at least little news of the forces overseas. By 1945, 58,000 copies a week were being distributed to the three Canadian services in Great Britain. Response to questionnaires had shown that the paper was much appreciated by its readers, though inevitably there were many suggestions for improvement, including some demand for comic strips. One commanding officer reported that all ranks would like the London *Daily Mirror*'s celebrated strip 'Jane,' whose heroine lost practically all her clothes practically every day.[52]

After the Canadian Army went into action on the Continent, a newspaper of its own was launched there. *The Maple Leaf* began publication in Italy in January 1944 and in Northwest Europe in July 1944. Edited by personnel of the Canadian Army Public Relations Groups in those theatres, it was a livelier paper than the *Canadian Press News*, had some editorial policy (which sometimes led to friction with the military authorities),

and ran such features as the famous 'Herbie' cartoons by W.G. ('Bing') Coughlin.[53] After VE-Day, since the Canadian Press did not wish to continue the *Canadian Press News*, it was decided to substitute a United Kingdom version of *The Maple Leaf* on a tri-service basis, 'for Canadian Forces in Britain.' This paper appeared first on 19 May 1945, and as a daily from 25 May.[54] It made a useful contribution to maintaining cheerfulness among the Canadians in England, Scotland, and Northern Ireland until it ceased publication in February 1946.

The Royal Canadian Air Force in Britain had its own weekly paper, *Wings Abroad*, produced beginning in April 1942 by the Public Relations staff at the RCAF's London headquarters.[55] This paper undoubtedly served as one means of maintaining a Canadian link with the enormous numbers of individual Canadians serving in Royal Air Force units, as well as with the RCAF squadrons scattered through the RAF.

And then there was radio, enormously important in people's lives in those days. Programming began early in 1940 with the British Broadcasting Corporation sending out once a week the final period of a National Hockey League game. It rapidly expanded, until by the end of the year the BBC was broadcasting regular short programs of Canadian news and sports prepared by its Canadian counterpart, the CBC. Three years later programming for the Canadians had grown to two hours and ten minutes each week. The most popular show was the half-hour Johnny Canuck's Revue, a variety show featuring soldier concert parties. It was also enjoyed by the British public and by British servicemen overseas. British listeners would write fan letters addressed to Mr Johnny Canuck, care of the

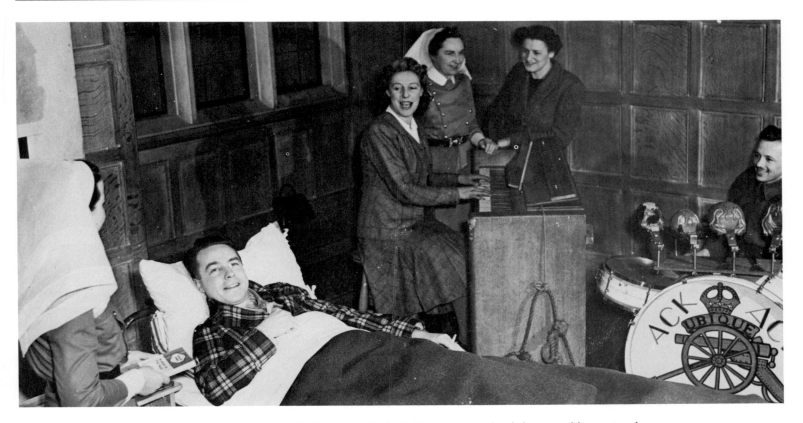

'Ack-Ack Annie,' otherwise known as Judy Dollman, entertained those unable to attend
concerts. Here she plays for patients at No 6 Canadian Casualty Clearing Station at Cranleigh,
Surrey, in December 1943. (DHist, DND, 27831)

A small Scottish citizen provides an audience outside Edinburgh Castle
for members of the RCAF show, the 'Blackouts,' then touring Scotland. (RCAF, PL 31865)

Members of the Canadian Army Show clowning at an RCAF field in the Netherlands, October 1944. Left to right, Staff Sergeant Frank Shuster, Sergeant Johnny Wayne, and Lance-Corporal Alf Wickbergh. (RCAF, PL 33303)

English playwright Noël Coward with Alan and Blanche Lund at the
Navy Show's London opening, February 1945. (F.R. Kemp, PAC / DND, PA 147134)

BBC. So popular was the revue in Britain that Captain Brian Meredith, the radio liaison officer at CMHQ, found it desirable to caution performers about one aspect of their material: 'On the whole, the less said about relationships between Canadian soldiers and the girls of this country, the better. Jokes may be laughed at at the time, but subconsciously they will contribute to worry in the minds of British troops overseas, and to Canadian listeners in Canada. They will both be jealous.'[56]

News from home took another and still more important form: letters from family and friends. Nothing was more vital to the morale of the service man or woman abroad than mail, and few problems were more difficult. In peacetime, mail had moved across the Atlantic smoothly and rapidly. Numbers of liners maintained fast and regular steamship service, and in 1939 transatlantic air service, and air mail with it, were just beginning. War disrupted all this. Regular sailings ended, liners were requisitioned to serve as transports, and enemy action took constant toll of Allied shipping. The only regular transoceanic air service to survive the outbreak of war was the American Clippers flying to neutral Lisbon. In these circumstances, getting mail to Canadian servicemen overseas with any speed and certainty was hard to compass, and it continued to be so for a long time. The war gave a great impetus to transatlantic flying, but it took time to produce regular and reliable mail service. The slowness and irregularity of mail from home was one of the chronic complaints of service people overseas. In the autumn of 1941 the censors in England reported, 'Most units are grumbling about the slowness of the mail in general, and there are many complaints about the non-arrival of mail.' One writer is quoted as saying, 'I will truly say dear, that if our mail is not better the boys can not last much longer. Walked through the camp today and 90 per cent were complaining of no mail. It is surprising the moral effect it has on them.'[57] Such references are legion.

The Canadian Postal Corps, which served all three Canadian armed services and had to grapple with all the problems of wartime transport, bore the brunt of criticism, much of it ignorant and unjustified. Gradually conditions improved. When the Royal Air Force Transport Command was set up to ferry bombers from Canada to Britain, arrangements were made for its planes to carry 'armed forces air letters,' single sheets similar to the air forms still in use. Beginning in November 1941, airgraph letters were introduced. This involved letters being microfilmed and sent overseas in this form, thus making maximum use of the limited air transport available. Ordinary surface letters, however, were still being sent by steamship, with all the possibilities of delay and destruction that this implied. As additional aircraft became available it was possible to form the Canadian Transatlantic Air Service, operated for the Canadian Department of Transport by Trans-Canada Air Lines (now Air Canada). The first eastbound flight was made on 22 July 1943, and scheduled flights soon began. After air mail had been loaded on these planes, the remaining space was filled with ordinary 'surface' letters to the forces overseas, which thus received air transmission without additional charge. By the end of hostilities with Germany all air and 'surface' mail to the Canadian forces overseas was in fact going by air. But as late as 1944 large quantities of mail were being lost by air accident or enemy action. On 28 December of that year the Canadian Transatlantic Air Service lost a Lancaster carrying mail from Canada to Britain. No trace of plane or crew was ever found.[58]

As a result of the authorities' efforts, the situation gradually improved. There is a report in July 1942 of an armed forces air letter reaching London from Ottawa in four days,[59] which must have been about an all-time record; but this sort of thing could not be counted on, and in the winter season particularly the service still tended to be slow.

The RCAF's mail problems were worse than the army's, which were bad enough. Getting letters to RCAF squadrons was comparatively easy; getting them to the thousands of Canadians serving as individuals in Royal Air Force units was a great deal harder. In September 1941 the Canadian Postal Corps asked RCAF Headquarters in London for additional personnel for the RCAF Section, Canadian Base Post Office, and was promised two additional clerks on loan. The record says,[60] 'Discussed what action should be taken to ascertain the actual number of R.C.A.F. personnel in the U.K., the R.A.F. Records Office in the first instance having passed over to the Canadian Base Post Office approximately 2700 names. The O.C. Canadian Base Post Office reports that on 3 Sept 41, 6215 names were on record, and that approximately 1500 additional names for which no locations could be found were also on hand, these names having been taken from Embarkation Lists and other sources. No suggestions were forthcoming.' One sympathizes with the overseas postal authorities who had to

bring order out of this chaos. In 1941 the graduates of the British Commonwealth Air Training Plan were beginning to arrive in Britain in large numbers, and it would take time to adjust to this situation.

In 1942 the strength of the Postal Corps overseas was much increased, and the RCAF insisted that a proportion of its personnel should change from khaki to air force blue. It is clear that great efforts were made to get mail promptly to the Canadians in the RAF, and clear also that troubles continued. Part of the difficulty arose from the failure of air force people to report their own changes of posting.[61] The situation improved with time and experience. Murray Peden, who arrived overseas at the end of 1942 and served in No 214 Squadron RAF, recalls, 'At the end of 1942 and the beginning of 1943 the blue air mail forms would come to us in about fifteen or sixteen days. I find that in one of my letters of that period I wrote home remarking on the fact that I had received one in as little as 12 days.' Heavy surface letters and ordinary air letters didn't as a rule do so well, and there was a good deal of irregularity and resulting complaint. The situation, in fact, was much the same as in the army.[62]

Education in the services was a means of providing that the members of the forces who were lucky enough to survive the war could return to civil life better equipped for its demands than when they enlisted. However, it served a more immediate purpose by keeping the troops usefully occupied at periods when military activity was largely suspended – which meant, particularly, in the winter. Soon after the outbreak of war the

The Waverley Hotel in Hastings, Sussex, was converted into a recreational centre for Canadian servicemen in June 1942. Here the club secretary, Mrs F. Goulding, is seen with an appreciative group of Canadian airmen. (A. Louis Jarché, DHist, DND, 7-22)

The Maple Leaf Club, London, whose roof garden is shown here,
was run by the Canadian Red Cross. (A. Louis Jarché, DHist, DND, 2676-20)

Canadian newspapers and magazines were one of the attractions of the Beaver Club,
the largest Canadian servicemen's club in London. (A. Louis Jarché, DHist, DND, 2659-5)

Canadian Legion War Services undertook the task of providing educational facilities for the forces. Robert England was appointed overseas director; but the feverish military activity of the summer of 1940 gave nobody any time to think of education, and England returned to Canada.[63] With the advent of autumn, and the decline of the invasion menace, everything changed. The pressing problem now was to give the troops occupation during the long blacked-out evenings of winter – occupation better than that offered by the pubs and brawling in the streets.

So far as the army was concerned, General McNaughton had no doubt as to the solution. An active educational program was required, and with characteristic energy he threw himself into the business of getting it organized. His papers reflect the steps he took.[64] Dr A.E. Chatwin arrived from Canada to succeed England on behalf of the Canadian Legion; but McNaughton was anxious to have a personal representative in the work, and fortunately the man was at hand in the person of J.B. Bickersteth, warden of Hart House at the University of Toronto, who was in England in the Home Guard. Bickersteth served McNaughton until 1942; when the British War Office snapped him up to become its director of education, Douglas LePan succeeded him. LePan has described his work – and, incidentally, the remarkable man he worked for – in a highly interesting memoir.[65] When he moved on in 1943 to become, shortly, a private soldier in the army, the organization was militarized under a director of education at CMHQ, Major, later Colonel, John Grace.

The actual work of education must be briefly summarized.

Three Canadians arriving in London at the beginning of their leave in January 1942. (DHist, DND, 5408)

Correspondence courses were important. The Canadian Legion had arranged for the compilation of booklets to serve as the basis for such courses in many subjects, including technical ones, to help soldiers gain credits at the primary or secondary school, and subsequently even at the university level. This program continued actively until the end of the war. There was also a program of 'directed reading,' less formal and not intended to obtain credits. Classes were organized in many units, often designed to assist men in improving their knowledge of technical subjects important to their duties. Unit education officers were appointed. It was found that these officers, usually junior, frequently changed, and often not greatly interested, tended to be ineffective; the provision of 'education corporals,' whose full time was devoted to the work, ultimately proved to be a more successful expedient. Units were encouraged to provide quiet reading rooms where men could study without interruption. Unit libraries were set up and arrangements made for books to be changed from time to time.[66]

The Canadians were not left entirely to their own resources. Britain's institutions of culture and learning were opened to them. Technical colleges and institutes accepted soldiers for study in off-duty hours. The Royal Institute of International Affairs at Chatham House, London, arranged courses in international relations for Canadian officers. The British Council, an organization whose object was the development of closer relations between the United Kingdom and other countries, was very helpful, arranging visits to farms, industrial and historic sites, and co-operating with the Canadian Legion in

A London policeman, complete with gas mask, gives Canadian soldiers on leave in London directions at the Marble Arch, January 1942. (DHist, DND, 570-18)

The Canadian high commissioner and Mrs Massey at the Canadian Legion Club
during a tour of clubs in London at Christmas, 1941. (DHist, DND, 5363)

A soldier of the Essex Scottish, on duty on England's south coast, uses his bayonet
to open a welcome package from Canada as Christmas approaches in 1941. (DHist, DND, 518-17)

organizing short leave courses in British universities.[67]

These courses, which began at Oxford and spread to many other universities, were enormously appreciated. Witness a letter written by a private in the Ordnance Corps: 'I attended a course at Balliol in Oxford. That is one of the 25 colleges that make up Oxford. There were about 82 persons attending, British, American and Canadian. I was practically the only private there – most were very high ranking officers. However, all differences in rank were forgotten while we were there.'[68] A Canadian who had studied at Oxford in peacetime had a chance of seeing the beginning of this program in 1942, and described it to his family:

I was tremendously pleased with what I saw at Oxford. It has taken the University a long time to get around to doing anything for our fellows (and I believe, actually, that this idea *began* with a scheme for the Yankees, that our people were then included, and the Yanks then, for the time at least, decided that this was not a good moment for them, so our people have it to themselves.) However this may be, it is succeeding very well, and I gather the Oxford people are no end pleased now that the ice is broken. Certainly they are treating our boys very well indeed; and as the groups of lads who are going are really very good people (mixed officers and other ranks, but chiefly the latter; and the quality is such as to make one quite proud of this army of ours) I think a real relationship of mutual regard is growing up as a result, and this is not invariably the consequence of such enterprises. The boys go in groups of forty; they are accommodated in colleges (Christ Church and Wadham), they are given a chance to attend a mild programme of lectures by experts on subjects of interest, and they get a proper but not overpowering amount of hospitality ... And there is no doubt that they have liked it and been very grateful, and that Oxford is delighted, so far, with the results of its bold experiment.[69]

This particular group was taken to Stratford-on-Avon, saw *The Merchant of Venice* at the Memorial Theatre, and was guided by a Stratford alderman on a tour of the town.

At the other end of the educational spectrum, illiterate men were being taught to read and write; an Education Company was organized for this purpose. Another project in the field of general education was the 'Pre-octu School,' intended to prepare potential officers for successful attendance at an Officer Cadet Training Unit. At the beginning of 1943 Mr LePan compiled a statistical summary of what the army had accomplished. It showed 3733 men then taking Canadian Legion correspondence courses, 1073 taking similar British courses, and 315 taking courses on the university level. Each month an average of 6000 men were attending classes, often in civilian schools. In the units, 18,734 men were taking part in a winter educational program, thanks largely to the activity of the education corporals. The University Short Courses just described had attracted 833 men. The Army Bureau of Current Affairs, a British invention in which Canadians had actively involved themselves, had held two weekend courses at Chatham House, each attended by about 300 Canadian officers. Lectures had attracted an average monthly attendance of 8000. Libraries being serviced numbered 587. More

General Wavell, the hero of the first Western Desert campaign,
looks down on Canadians enjoying their tea at a recreation centre at Eastbourne, Sussex.
(A. Louis Jarché, DHist, DND, 3-15)

Education officer's tent, with bulletins on progress
of the war, February 1944. (G. Barry Gilroy, PAC / DND, PA 150137)

than 1000 requests per month were received for guidance in directed reading. St John Ambulance First Aid Classes had led to 1024 certificates being issued.[70] It was a remarkable record. The program had contributed to combatting boredom in a long-idle army; it had fitted men to be both better soldiers and better citizens; and it had been one more influence bringing Canadians and the British people closer together.

After the Canadian Army went into action, the educational service in Britain largely lost its occupation, though it still had customers in the Reinforcement Units, the hospitals, and various static units. When the Germans surrendered, however, education again became important, to combat boredom among the troops awaiting repatriation and to help men and women prepare themselves for the return to civil life. Now – in imitation of an institution set up after the earlier war – the Khaki University of Canada came into being. It had three branches: the Junior College, University Extension, and Vocational Extension. The Junior College was residential, and ran three-month courses at first- and second-year university level, the objects being to assist students to prepare themselves for entering upon, or resuming, university studies and, 'in appropriate cases,' to give them an opportunity to write examinations leading to credits at a recognized Canadian university. The other branches provided for study in British or continental institutions, or through professional or other associations in the United Kingdom, at the student's expense. The president of the university was Brigadier G.E. Beament, a University of Toronto graduate and a lawyer in civil life, and the faculty, except for selected people brought from Canada, were found from among qualified members of the Canadian Army Overseas.[71]

The Khaki University's headquarters and Junior College were established at Leavesden, near Watford, northwest of London. It was co-educational; a women's residence accommodated twenty students. A visitor described the establishment in September 1945: 'It is now functioning on a large scale and presents an impressive appearance. Distinctions of rank have virtually been swept away; all students wear plain battle-dress with the K.U. flash, and living conditions are the same for officers and O.RS. Students' sleeping quarters are double rooms in all cases. There is quite a good library [many of the books were loaned by the British Council] and a well-equipped chemical laboratory. The main idea is to provide conditions that will cushion the shock of the change from army life to a civilian university: Brigadier Beament has sought to reproduce, in effect, a Canadian university in the United Kingdom.'[72] The Khaki University completed two three-month Junior College courses before the repatriation of its potential students brought it to an end in the late spring of 1946.[73]

The other services' situations were quite different from that of the army. Navy personnel, we have said, were in general birds of passage in the United Kingdom; naval men's needs while their ships were in British ports were for rest and recreation, and if the educational services could provide them with light reading it was as much as they were likely to expect. As for the air force, Britain was for it a theatre of active operations, and men in operational squadrons were unlikely

A.P. Herbert, MP, eminent author, and petty officer in the Naval Auxiliary Patrol,
conducts a tour of the Thames as part of a short course run for Canadian service people by the
University of London, July 1942. (C.E. Nye, PAC / DND, PA 147109)

to have a problem of boredom, or the time and inclination to improve their standard of education. The record does not indicate that the RCAF overseas had any very active educational program.

Organized recreation – organized officially or unofficially – undoubtedly did a good deal to keep Canadian service people agreeably occupied and contented during the long sojourn in Britain. Nevertheless, it seems likely that unofficial hospitality and private friendship, the gifts of innumerable British families, did more. They are still well remembered after many years.

CHAPTER FIVE

Lonely Canadians, British Women

IN JUNE 1942 the Canadian high commissioner and Mrs Massey, driving back to London from a trip to the country, picked up a Canadian soldier and an English girl in the Women's Auxiliary Air Force, who sat in front with the chauffeur. Massey later recorded, 'They seemed tremendously in love with each other'; but the chauffeur had informed him 'that they had just met waiting for a bus!'[1] This anecdote may serve to introduce the very large subject of relations between the sexes in wartime Britain.

The many thousands of Canadian men whom the war brought to the country were most of them young and possessed of the normal sexual instincts. Many were single; those who were married had been obliged to leave their wives at home. In the early months, it is true, a certain number of Canadian wives came to England to be with their husbands; though in the nature of things this was possible only for the comparatively wealthy. Mrs McNaughton and Mrs Crerar both came, and Mrs McNaughton stayed until her husband returned to Canada after losing the army command. But the critical war situation in the summer of 1940 led the Canadian government to pass an order-in-council forbidding Canadian women to travel to war zones except on official duty.[2] Thereafter, a serviceman going overseas was even more completely separated from his family in Canada.

In Britain, family life was disrupted as it was in Canada, only more so because of Britain's deeper involvement in the war. Husbands and fathers were serving in distant countries. Great numbers of young women left home to engage in war work: in the women's services, in munition factories, or on the land. Normal social restraints were relaxed. The adjutant general of the British Army, General Sir Ronald Adam, wrote to his friend McNaughton in the course of a discussion of mutual problems in 1943, 'The morals of the British have deteriorated as a result of the war – there is no getting away from that fact.'[3] Even before the war Britain's was a more permissive society than Canada's, and the wartime community into which the Canadians were thrust was more permissive than Britain had been before 1939, in sexual matters as in others. Britain was still Britain; it would be absurd to say that all British social standards had gone by the board; but a country conducting a

'They ain't got nothin' our girls haven't got, only they've got it here!'

Herbie, the creation of Bing Coughlin, was a popular character who appeared regularly in *The Maple Leaf*, the newspaper of the Canadian Army Overseas. (Reproduced by permission Director Information Services, DND)

total war of defence against a ruthless enemy only a score of miles away is bound to undergo great changes.

In the autumn of 1943 the senior Roman Catholic chaplain of the Canadian Reinforcement Units recorded 'points discussed with New Drafts from Canada,' and they dealt mainly with relations with English women.[4] These he divided into three main classes. First were the prostitutes: 'More common than at home. Cold, calculating lot. Interested in your pocket book. VD prevalent. Here they are not obliged to seek medical treatment as they are at home. Hardly necessary to waste time talking about them. You do not have to meet them. They will meet you. Beware.' The second class hardly any name suited. 'Working girls, factory, munitions etc. Probably away from their own homes. They will entertain you and they are serious about it. If they had any morals, they have discarded them. But first, as they invite you to have a beer or lunch or to a dance, they will also suggest you stay all night. These are very dangerous because they take you unawares.' The third class were the 'Good Girls': 'This is the last class you will meet. You won't find them in pubs, etc., but usually in their own homes. Naturally they are the last ones you meet, because they are not always on the street. When you meet them, treat them as you would treat your best girl at home, or as you want English, Australian or other airmen training in Canada, to treat your sisters and sweethearts.' Like many other chaplains, and other people in authority, this padre advised against wartime marriages, remarking, 'There are at least two divorce cases a week being handled at CMHQ. These are ones we know about.'

How much attention this chaplain's young parishioners at

the Reinforcement Units paid to his advice generally is a question that remains unanswered. Certain it is that on the particular matter of marriage he and his colleagues were fighting a losing battle.

The first marriage between a Canadian soldier and a British woman took place in Farnborough Church in the Aldershot area as early as 29 January 1940, not much more than a month after the first flight of the 1st Division came up the Clyde; the bridegroom was a company sergeant-major of the Saskatoon Light Infantry.[5] There were 1221 more marriages to Canadian officers and soldiers that year. Thereafter the number continued to grow, in the face of official discouragement. In the beginning the army regulation simply stipulated that permission must be granted by the soldier's commanding officer before the bride could receive dependants' allowance.[6] In the RCAF, ground crew had to complete six months' service before they could obtain permission and the allowance, but this did not apply overseas. This condition did not apply to aircrew anywhere. There were no regulations for naval personnel.[7]

In November 1940 new regulations were issued for the Canadian Army Overseas. Henceforth, subalterns and warrant officers under the age of twenty, and all non-commissioned officers and men, needed their commanding officers' permission to marry. Moreover, men under nineteen, and their fiancées, if under twenty-one, required the written consent of parents or guardians. Commanding officers were instructed not to grant permission unless they were satisfied that the soldier applicant realized his financial responsibility and was free from debt, and that the prospective bride was of good moral character. An amendment reminded Canadians that 'the validity of a marriage is governed by compliance with the laws of the country in which the marriage takes place.'[8]

Canadian commanders, reflecting no doubt that a troublesome marriage might affect a soldier's morale and fighting value, did their best to discourage hasty alliances. In 1941 chaplains in the Canadian Corps were urged to use their influence in this direction. Some women, it was suggested, might marry Canadians merely to get the dependants' allowance.[9] A staff officer at CMHQ reminded his superiors of the possible burden on Canadian taxpayers: 'There is the future pension liability and the problem of transporting the wives (and children) back to Canada; and the probability that some of them will not fit into Canadian life and will thus become a burden on the public.' 'It might also be considered that each marriage overseas is robbing some Canadian girl of a husband.'[10]

A further tightening of the army marriage regulations in December 1941 may well have been the result of bigamous marriages coming to light. It was now required that a soldier applying for permission to marry declare his current marital status, his 'probable ability to maintain family after discharge,' and his consent to a $10 monthly deduction from his pay until $200 was accumulated. This would be used to pay for his family's passage to Canada. His fiancée needed a certificate from a 'responsible citizen' attesting to her good character, and a two-month waiting period was imposed before the wedding could take place.[11] Commanding officers were instructed to impress upon applicants 'the seriousness of the proposed step and the permanency of marriage having regard to the fact that

RCAF men and a guest enjoy punting,
a popular local pastime on the Yorkshire river Nidd, July 1944. (RCAF, PL 31597)

it can be dissolved only by the courts.'[12] In practice, this duty usually fell to the unit chaplain, and, frequently, it was the chaplain who was expected to provide the woman's character reference. This was not always easy; indeed, there were times when he was asked to certify that a woman, already pregnant by the prospective groom, was of good character. Chaplains found themselves increasingly taken up with such matters. One estimated that half his time was spent in marriage counselling.[13] Some of the cases referred to the padres were so difficult and entangled that they defied a satisfactory – let alone a happy – solution. In one, the wife of a British soldier serving overseas sought support for one of her three children who had been fathered by a Canadian soldier. The Canadian had already applied for permission to marry another woman 'and his mother is dependent on him so that financially he is getting himself into deep water.'[14] Another chaplain had to tell a pregnant fiancée that the prospective groom was already married and the father of three children.[15] No doubt, as is usually the case, it was the unfortunate and sensational affairs like these that were recorded; the numerous normal and respectable marriages passed without comment.

It's hardly surprising that Roman Catholic chaplains actively discouraged marriage of Catholic soldiers with non-Catholics. And commanding officers of French-speaking units sometimes took the same attitude towards marriage with English women. One woman complained to CMHQ in September 1941 that the commanding officer of Les Fusiliers Mont-Royal had refused permission for her fiancé to marry her because he opposed such marriages on principle.[16] He was not alone. It was reported in January 1943 that there had yet to be a marriage of a member of Le Régiment de la Chaudière in Britain – and the regiment had been there since August 1941.[17]

When the bulk of the Canadian Army moved to the Continent the effort to discourage marriages was stepped up. Canadian Army North West Europe Routine Order No 788 stated that the general policy was to 'dissuade members of the Canadian Army from a marriage in foreign lands,' but it was no more effective than the efforts in Britain. This may be the place to record the impressive statistics of Canadian marriages overseas. The grand total of marriages of Canadian service personnel in Great Britain to the end of 1946 was 44,886.[18] In some cases, of course, the marriage was between Canadians, or between a Canadian and a partner who was not British; but the vast majority were between Canadian men and British women. And the marriages were fruitful; the number of children by 31 December 1946 was 21,358.[19]

It is interesting to note the periods of the war at which most marriages took place. There were 1222 in 1940. As the number of Canadians in the United Kingdom increased, so did the number of weddings: 3011 in 1941, 4160 in 1942, 5897 in 1943. The latter year saw many Canadian soldiers leaving for Italy, and from June 1944 great numbers were fighting in Northwest Europe. There were 3927 marriages in the first half of that year, but only 2273 in the second. There are no figures for January 1945, but the four months February-May saw 2402 marriages. The war in Europe ended in May, and the movement of the fighting soldiers back to England and on to Canada began at once. During the repatriation process large

An early group of wives and children of Canadian servicemen
embark for their new homes, April 1944. (W.J. Hynes, PAC / DND, PA 147114)

numbers of them were married in England: in the seven months May-November, 5814, including 1367 in August alone.[20] Among the newlyweds were some repatriated prisoners of war.[21]

The continental country that provided most Canadian war brides was the Netherlands, where large numbers of Canadian soldiers spent the summer of 1945. By the end of 1946 there had been 1886 Canadian marriages to Dutch women. There were 649 Belgian brides, 100 French, 6 German, 7 Danish, and 26 Italian.[22]

In Britain an effort was made to help the new Canadians prepare themselves for the difficult transition to the different life of North America. As early as September 1941 a thoughtful chaplain, Honorary Captain J.I. McKinney, had formed a Maple Leaf Club in West Wickham, Kent, for the wives of soldiers of the 3rd Field Regiment, RCA. In 1943 Princess Alice Clubs – named for the royal wife of the governor general of Canada, the Earl of Athlone – came into existence at Chichester and Brighton. At first the response was reported to be slight; according to one chaplain, 'the majority of the young wives ... have no interest in Canada.'[23] In 1944 things improved. One reason was better Canadian organization. The Immigration Branch of the Department of Mines and Resources was in charge of moving servicemen's dependants to Canada in the first instance, and 1160 wives and 576 children were sent off before April 1944. A considerable number of the brides thus reached their new country before their husbands returned to it, and no doubt they encountered many problems. In August 1944 the Department of National Defence assumed

A soldier of the Royal Canadian Army Pay Corps with his English wife and child, photographed in London in March 1943. (Towers, PAC / DND, PA 154978)

the responsibility. The army took on the job for all three services, and a Canadian Wives Bureau was set up as a directorate of the Adjutant-General's Branch at CMHQ.[24]

The bureau, in addition to arranging the dependants' passages to Canada, encouraged the formation of more clubs where the wives could hold social gatherings and hear talks on life in Canada. The Salvation Army gave active assistance, and by November 1945 there were thirty-two such clubs functioning in England and Scotland. After most of the service personnel had been repatriated, the great movement of dependants began in February 1946. Between August 1944 and January 1947, when the responsibility of transporting the remaining few was passed back from National Defence to the Immigration Branch and the Department of Veterans Affairs, 61,088 dependants were moved from the United Kingdom and Northwest Europe to Canada; and the vast majority were from Britain. There were 33,264 army wives with 16,987 children; 7197 wives and 2466 children of the RCAF; while the navy's share was 890 wives and 284 children.[25]

Characteristically, British commentators are surprised to discover that more brides from Britain went to Canada than to the United States. An official British analysis notes, 'At the time public interest was concentrated on the arrangements made for those who were popularly known as "G.I. Brides," yet in fact it was the dependants of Canadian servicemen who provided the largest number of travellers ... over 40,000 wives and nearly 20,000 children, as compared with 34,000 wives and 14,000 children of United States servicemen. Over half the American wives were between 20 and 24 years of age at the time of sailing, and over half the children they took with them were less than one year old. The age distribution of the Canadian brides is not known, but the average age of their children was noticeably higher than that of the American children. The reason for these differences ... becomes apparent when it is remembered that Canadian forces were stationed in this country early in the war, but that the American forces did not start arriving here until about three years later.'[26]

It is hardly the business of this book to attempt the more-than-Herculean task of telling the story of the fortunes of the war brides in Canada. Every individual's experience was different, and they ranged from the idyllic to the tragic. But there is no doubt that the war brought to Canada many British women who proved to be great assets to the country.* One example may suffice. Betty Oliphant was a war bride. Her marriage did not last. But 'Miss O' became the head and inspiration of the National Ballet School, and made a distinguished and unique contribution to Canadian culture.[27]

The Canadians in Britain in 1939–45 were of course not all

---

*In The War Brides (Toronto 1978), Joyce Hibbert collected some sixty women's stories of their experiences. This small sample leaves a rather grim impression, due, perhaps, to the fact that so many of the writers happened to marry into French families where the language barrier was a serious problem, and/or found themselves on primitive frontier farms. Once again, perhaps, it is the unfortunate who are voluble; the many whose experiences were happy do not write. But it is a notable fact that so many who had early troubles affirm that they would not now want to live in any country but Canada.

males. There were some Canadian women in the country when war broke out; as we have seen, some wives with husbands in the services followed them overseas in the early days; and after the Canadian government got around to authorizing the formation of women's branches of the forces, considerable numbers of their members served in the United Kingdom.

The first draft of the Canadian Women's Army Corps reached England in November 1942. By the end of the war with Germany, 1984 all ranks had served in the European zone; of these, 313 – Canadians living in the country, or wives of Canadian servicemen – had been appointed or enlisted in Britain. A fair number – it's impossible to say how many – of the women had husbands in the services; the possibility of joining a husband overseas certainly attracted some recruits to the various women's corps. On 30 April 1945 there were sixty-two officers and 1268 other ranks of the CWAC in Britain. They were employed chiefly at Canadian Military Head-quarters in London and at the Reinforcement Units in the Aldershot area. Nearly a thousand more CWAC women arrived overseas after VE-Day.[28]

The Women's Division of the RCAF appeared in Britain a little earlier than the CWAC, in September 1942. By 30 April 1945 its strength there had risen to 101 officers and 1239 airwomen. They worked at the RCAF overseas headquarters in London, at the headquarters of the RCAF Bomber Group, and at Linton and other RCAF stations. In London, unlike the CWAC who lived in barracks, the WDS were billeted in groups of two to four in approved lodgings.[29] The Women's Royal Canadian Naval Service also served in Britain, its total strength there being 503. They were chiefly in London, Greenock, and Londonderry.[30] The great majority of CWAC women overseas were employed in various forms of clerical work, relieving men for active service. There were other miscellaneous jobs (we have mentioned laundry workers) and, at the top of the scale, some CWAC women were trained as staff officers for duty in various headquarters.

Last but not least were the nursing sisters, all of whom were officers. They inherited a tradition from the First World War, and indeed from earlier conflicts. In the beginning the Royal Canadian Army Medical Corps served all three of the Cana-dian forces, but as the war proceeded the RCAF and RCN organized their own medical services, inevitably including nursing sisters (later termed by the navy 'nursing officers'). Large numbers of women from all three forces served in Britain, chiefly in hospitals. The army's nursing service over-seas rose to a strength of 2263. In November 1944 there were ten RCAMC general hospitals in the United Kingdom and twelve on the Continent. As a result of the RCAF's close integration with the RAF, there were no RCAF hospitals in Britain. The navy had one, at HMCS *Niobe* at Greenock.[31]

Canadian women also served in the United Kingdom in non-military organizations. The Canadian Red Cross Corps and the St John Ambulance Brigade were authorized to do voluntary work in Canadian hospitals abroad, their members paying their own way to Britain and their own expenses. The Red Cross ran four hostels for Canadian servicemen in London. The Mechanized Transport Corps and the Women's Transport Service, both British organizations, were allowed to

A group of war brides in the lounge at the
Canadian Wives' Bureau, London, November 1944. (C.H. Richer, PAC / DND, PA 147115)

Members of the Canadian Women's Army Corps in London
decorate the Christmas tree in their quarters, 1942. (PAC / DND, PA 129085)

The Canadian Women's Army Corps' first softball game of the season,
Hyde Park, London, May 1943. (Dwight E. Dolan, PAC / DND, PA 150133)

Members of the RCAF Women's Division in their quarters at the
headquarters of the RCAF Bomber Group, February 1944. (RCAF, PL 26754)

Members of the RCAF Women's Division (in white) play 'mud football' against their sisters
of the Royal Norwegian Air Force in Hyde Park, March 1944. Norway won. (RCAF, PL 29100)

recruit in Canada, and small numbers of Canadian women went overseas wearing their uniforms – and also at their own expense.[32]

Even taking them all together, however, the women were obviously a small proportion of the Canadian wartime community in Britain. The Canadian serviceman seeking female companionship usually found it among British women.

The great number of marriages represent what may be called the bright side of the story of the relations of Canadian servicemen with British women. There was also a dark side.

Part of it was bigamy. There is no way of telling just how many bigamous marriages Canadians contracted in Britain during the war, but ten cases were prosecuted in military courts and twelve in British civil courts to August 1945.[33] There were undoubtedly a good many more. Canadian soldiers whose wives in Canada were not getting dependants' allowance could easily pass themselves off as single men, and the Canadian authorities were well aware of this. We have noted that new marriage regulations issued in December 1941 required the soldier to declare his current marital status; but it was virtually impossible to verify such statements overseas, especially since marriage records were maintained by the provinces rather than centrally, and a marriage performed in another province would not be recorded in a man's province of residence. And if a soldier declared himself to be a widower the statement was virtually impossible to check – unless of course he himself produced a death certificate, a procedure which could hardly be insisted upon.

There was also the question of illegitimate children fathered by Canadian servicemen. Nobody knows how many there were. We do know, however, that 414 maintenance orders were brought to the attention of CMHQ by British civil courts to August 1945, that there were 283 voluntary assignments by Canadian soldiers in favour of their illegitimate children, and 144 awards made to such children by the Dependants' Allowance Board.[34] There seems to be no record of cases in which RCAF or RCN personnel were involved. Jean Ellis, who served with the Canadian Red Cross in London, has described some of the problems presented by unmarried mothers. For instance, the Red Cross provided a layette for every child of a Canadian serviceman, legitimate or otherwise. But paternity had to be proved, and it wasn't always easy; the Red Cross tried hard, but there were cases where all the mother could report was that she thought the father's first name was, for instance, Joe![35]

The high commissioner and Canadian military authorities were acutely aware of the problem of caring for these children, especially after the Canadian forces left Britain. At the same time, it seemed hardly practicable for the Canadian government to assume responsibility and seek to make Canadian veterans, at home with their families, provide support for bastard children in Britain. Early in 1946 at least a partial solution presented itself. The Toronto *Evening Telegram*, a newspaper that had been very active in patriotic endeavours during the war, had sponsored a British War Victims Fund which had done much for British people who had suffered by bombing or otherwise. There was £11,235 in British money remaining in the fund at the end of the war, and the *Telegram* offered this 'for the immediate relief ... of the children, legitimate or otherwise,' of Canadians who had served in Britain. Mr Massey convened a meeting at Canada House at which representatives of the three services, the Canadian Red Cross, the immigration authorities, and the Department of Veterans Affairs agreed that the offer should be accepted and that Veterans Affairs should administer the fund. Alan Chambers, district administrator of DVA in Britain, took charge of it and, while the money lasted, grants-in-aid were made 'in cases of necessity not otherwise provided for by the public legislation.' Chambers also administered a fund of £5000 donated earlier by W.A. Black of Montreal to assist distressed servicemen and persons connected with them.[36]

Venereal disease is a problem in every military force, and the Canadians in Britain in 1939–45 were no exception. In December 1939, when the arrival of the 1st Division was imminent, Lieutenant-Colonel (later Major-General) R.M. Luton, director of medical services at the new Canadian Military Headquarters in London, asked what preventive measures were taken by the British War Office in Aldershot and London. The reply was that prophylactic packets *should* be available, that preventive ablution rooms *should* be set up, and that lectures on VD should be given by medical and regimental officers. It was evident that the War Office expected the Canadians to make their own arrangements. This perhaps was fair enough; but Luton had another concern – the lack of legislation in Great Britain, such as existed in most Canadian provinces, which required persons known to be infected with VD to submit to treatment. He found that no such legislation was contemplated, although he knew that a belated regulation had been issued, under the Defence of the Realm Act, towards the end of the First World War. However, since by the middle of April 1940 only three cases of VD had been reported among the Canadian troops, it was decided that, at least for the moment, the matter need not be raised with the British government.[37]

The fact that during the Canadians' first six months in Britain only 356 cases of VD (6.29 per cent of all hospital admissions) were reported led to a certain amount of complacency. There were no prophylactic centres and no VD lectures. However, by May 1941 the Canadian medical authorities were sufficiently disturbed to form a committee on venereal diseases. It recommended that lectures to small groups of men and fortnightly 'short-arm' inspections be instituted immediately and that condoms be provided at a nominal price.[38] It was time. Sixty VD cases were admitted to hospital in July 1941, and in September 241 cases were reported in the 1st Canadian Corps.[39] In October a 200-bed special hospital for VD cases was opened.[40] There still was no British legislation, but Luton was optimistic. In 1940 the Canadian Army had begun passing information on VD sources to the Ministry of Health, and the ministry had, in turn, 'applied pressure to the county authorities concerned to extend treatment facilities.' By August 1941 it appeared that the Ministries of Health and Labour were ready to press for greater control of the problem.[41] At the year's end, Luton reported that the annual rate of VD among Canadian troops was 30.72 per 1000 men and that the monthly total had increased steadily until it reached a peak in August and September.[42]

The Canadian Army opened a prophylactic centre in London in April 1942, primarily for soldiers on leave, and by June had centres in Edinburgh, Glasgow, and Brighton as well. At these establishments men could seek immediate treatment after 'exposure.' It would be a pity not to quote Sir Andrew Macphail's remark in his history of the Canadian medical services in the first war: 'To these men brought up in the poverty, chastity and obedience of the army, a large civilian city presented itself as a huge place of temptation, and many fell away from their good resolution.' By the end of 1942 the VD rate per thousand troops had risen to 33.8 and was described as 'the biggest problem amongst the so-called preventable diseases.'[43]

The brightest element in the picture was the introduction by the British government late in December 1942 of Defence Regulation 33B, which required anyone named by two or more persons as a possible source of VD infection to be examined and, if necessary, to undergo treatment. The Canadians still felt that everyone suffering from VD should be obliged to take treatment, but they were relieved that some progress had been made.[44]

On 16 April 1943 the problem of venereal disease in Britain was discussed at a meeting at the Home Office of British government and police officials and US and Canadian officers. The chief subject was relations between the Americans and British women, but Brigadier A.W. Beament of CMHQ had an opportunity to express the Canadian view that Regulation 33B did not go far enough. The meeting resulted in the formation of a Joint Committee on Venereal Diseases, which met for the first time on 25 June and decided that the regulation should not be altered 'as it had not been in operation long enough to draw any definite conclusions.'[45]

The VD rate per 1000 Canadian troops jumped from 33.8 in 1942 to 40.6 in 1943.[46] A full-scale educational offensive was now launched. Films, posters, and pamphlets, shipped from Canada for distribution overseas, told the men 'in simple language the "how" and "why" of venereal disease' and that 'prostitutes, pick-ups and promiscuous women' were its spreaders.[47] An order in July 1944 directed that 'instruction in the nature and prevention of venereal disease will be included in the regular training syllabus for all male personnel.'[48]

General Luton reported in August 1944 that the rate for the first quarter of the year had dropped to 31.8 per 1000 and for the second quarter to 22.4. He attributed this decline to the education program, to intensified training, the cessation in May of leave prior to D-Day, the subsequent departure of many troops for France, and 'the influence of the expanded VD control and the assistance of VD Control Officers.'[49] The rate of incidence in the United Kingdom for the whole of 1944 was a respectable 30.5 per 1000.[50] A particularly bright spot was the Canadian Women's Army Corps. In the period July-December 1944 there was only one established case of VD among members of the CWAC overseas. This, it was truly remarked, 'clearly demonstrates the high standard of character and intelligence of the Women's Corps.'[51]

The good news continued into the first quarter of 1945 when a rate of 25.4 was recorded – and this included patients in Britain who had been exposed to VD on the Continent. The venereal disease control officer at CMHQ cautioned that there was 'a natural tendency for a "seasonal" fall during the winter and early spring months.'[52] He was right. The rate for the second quarter – which saw the end of the fighting in Europe – jumped to 44.1. Still worse was to come. The increase was blamed on the return to Britain of troops from Northwest Europe where the incidence of VD had risen to 'truly alarming levels.' A second factor was the reaction to the cessation of hostilities, which 'led to a wave of celebration and sexual promiscuity' in the United Kingdom.[53] The appalling figures for the rest of 1945 – rates of 90.1 in the third quarter and 108.3 in the fourth – could probably be attributed in great part to the presence of patients who had been infected on the Continent, where in June the Canadian rate actually rose to 144 per 1000. Little, in a medical sense, could be done to reduce the incidence. The CMHQ VD control officer observed that the men were completely bored during their long wait for repatriation; the only solution was to get 'these dispirited men' to a normal environment as soon as possible. But, he wrote grimly, 'unless their economic security and opportunities to advance themselves in civilian life are provided in the manner which they have long looked forward to, the continued incidence of venereal disease among the civilian population of Canada presents an ominous picture.'[54] Fortunately, his fears were not realized.*

The impact of venereal disease in the Royal Canadian Air Force overseas is described in the Canadian medical services' official history. The statistics come from monthly reports made by RCAF Overseas Headquarters and presumably include all the Canadian airmen scattered through RAF units, but their completeness must be a matter of question. They show that the incidence of VD among male RCAF personnel in Britain was '75 to 100% higher than it was in Canada.' The rate per thousand male personnel (there are no figures for the Women's Division) peaked at 75.9 in 1945 compared with 62.1 for 1944.[55] No distinction is made between aircrew and groundcrew.

British records[56] distinguish between aircrew and groundcrew, and between commands of the RAF. They show that except in the earliest part of the war, VD was more prevalent in Bomber Command than in any other RAF command, and that it was commoner in No 6 (RCAF) Group than in any other bomber group. The director general of medical services at the Air Ministry reported in July 1943 that for the period March-May 1943 the incidence of VD in Bomber Command as a whole was 15.2 per thousand per annum; this includes both aircrew and groundcrew. No 6 Group's figure was 33.5; next came No 1,

---

*According to the *Canada Year Book*, provincial departments of health reported 38,772 cases of VD in 1944, 40,528 in 1945, 41,556 in 1946, and 33,476 in 1947.

which had 'about 1,200 Poles' (29.7), and No 93, with 'about 1,000 Poles' (17.3).[57] Another report, for January-May 1943, gives the figures for 'Canadians in Bomber Command' (not merely 6 Group?) as 58.0 for aircrew and 21.7 for ground personnel. The figures for the command as a whole were 37.2 and 9.6, respectively.[58]

When 'Bomber' Harris, Bomber Command's commander-in-chief, was informed of the situation, he issued on 9 January 1943 a violent instruction to all his group commanders concerning VD among aircrew: 'In future ... it will be the rule that anyone contracting Venereal Disease, irrespective of the stage he has reached in his operational tour, will be required to start afresh and complete his 30 sorties as soon as he is in a fit state of health so to do.' This order caused alarm at the Air Ministry, which insisted that it should be cancelled forthwith.[59]

It was generally agreed that the exceptional strain and danger of Bomber Command's operations against Germany were responsible for the situation. About the social circumstances in England contributing to it there was only speculation. Air Chief Marshal Sir Philip Joubert de la Ferté, who was asked to investigate the problem, referred in a letter of 13 September 1943 to the influence of 'the infecting of the immoral young women who abound in our large towns by the alien influx into this country since August 1940.'[60] On the same date he wrote, after inspecting three 'bad stations': 'I think there is enough on these three stations to point to two facts. One is, if you don't keep aircrew fully employed the whole time and well disciplined they will get into trouble, and the second is

that the situation as regards the R.C.A.F. Group is quite deplorable.'

In a joint report which Joubert made in collaboration with the eminent physician Lord Amulree,[61] they wrote of the women concerned, 'These women are mostly amateurs [that is, not professional prostitutes] and many are working in factories. There is also a growing number of young girls between 16 and 18 who find life both amusing and profitable in the company of aircrew both British and Allied who have plenty of money and few scruples.' It was evident that there was a connection between drunkenness and promiscuity, and Amulree remarked that women visiting bars 'are frequently persuaded by relatively wealthy American and Canadian troops to drink spirits rather than beer.'

The suggestion that the women had been infected by the 'alien influx' is hardly provable. So far as the Canadians are concerned, it seems unlikely that the high-school youngsters who made up the bulk of the Commonwealth Air Training Plan product really played a great part in infecting the 'immoral young women' of England – particularly since VD was so much more common among the RCAF in Britain than it was in Canada. However, the British convinced themselves that the outsiders were to blame. Lord Amulree wrote:

In a number of areas visited there was an opinion that venereal infection is conveyed very largely by Canadian, American, Polish and other Allied troops. This is explained partly in a very natural way that these men are foreigners in a strange country and any sexual intercourse in which they indulge must be extra-marital, partly because the first two certainly have a considerable amount of money to spend and can rapidly skim the top off the market, partly because the standard of treatment among foreign troops is not up to our own, and partly because of the irresistible fascination of the foreigner. The infection is given by these men and then our troops, etc., get infected themselves.[62]

This opinion is speculation, but it would be surprising if the 'foreign' invasion did not have some influence on the situation.

In August 1941 the British minister of health, Ernest Brown, had approached the air minister, Sir Archibald Sinclair, on the problem, suggesting the possibility of a defence regulation that would allow local medical officers of health to require persons whom two independent witnesses believed had infected them to submit to examination or treatment. As we have seen, the Canadian army favoured action along these lines. Brown remarked, 'we must necessarily feel a heavy responsibility towards the Dominion troops in this country.' Sinclair did not sympathize. He replied, 'I am not moved by a feeling of special responsibility for the Canadian troops as the incidence of venereal disease among the civil population in Canada is far higher than here.* We do, indeed, feel serious

*Sinclair seems to have been right. The *Canada Year Book* for 1946, the first to publish vᴅ statistics, gives the number of cases reported by provincial health departments for 1944 as 38,772. The British figure for 1944, for a much larger population, was 43,193: see Sir Arthur S. MacNalty, ed., *The Civilian Health and Medical Services*, 1 (London 1953), 116.

concern for the help [health?] of our own men in Canada' (he meant trainees under the Air Training Plan). However, he was prepared to go along with Brown's scheme, though with no great enthusiasm.[63] As we have seen, the proposed action was not taken until December 1942, when the arrival of large numbers of American troops (more important in the eyes of the British government than the Canadians) had given new urgency to the problem.

Joubert and Amulree had recommended an approach to 'the Office of the Dominion of Canada' and the air officer commanding the ʀᴄᴀꜰ overseas with a view to 'an improvement in the discipline and self-control' of ʀᴄᴀꜰ personnel 'in the autonomous Canadian Organisations in the United Kingdom.' The autonomy of those organizations was in fact quite limited, and neither Canada House nor the ʀᴄᴀꜰ Overseas Headquarters was really in a position to act with effect. No approach to them seems to have been made. The vᴅ situation in the ʀᴄᴀꜰ overseas does not seem to have changed much after 1943. At any rate, the incidence in the force at large did not vary greatly. As we have already seen, the rate rose in 1945, though less disastrously than in the army.[64]

The Royal Canadian Navy's problem with venereal disease in the United Kingdom was not nearly so serious as in the army or the air force. Naval personnel were much less numerous and there was frequent rotation to Canada. Perhaps because of the rising rate in Canada, the ʀᴄɴ sent its vᴅ control officer to Britain in the fall of 1944 to report on conditions there. He found the situation aboard visiting Canadian ships in the

Portsmouth area 'most encouraging,' while at Plymouth the VD rate was 'not excessive' at an estimated thirty per 1000 per annum. The rate in HMCS *Niobe*, the RCN's manning pool at Greenock, was higher and he attributed this to 'the proximity of Glasgow and other areas where a great deal of venereal disease is known to be present.' But he noted that the rates for naval personnel in Britain were, on the whole, lower than in Canada at approximately seventeen per thousand for the last six months of 1944.[65] Probably as a result of these findings, Naval Service Headquarters in Ottawa felt that there was no need for further reports from Britain.

Great numbers of the men of the Canadian forces who came to Britain had left wives in Canada. As the years passed, prolonged separation subjected these marriages to an almost intolerable strain. Malicious gossips, sometimes writing anonymous letters, made things worse, telling the husband overseas that his wife was 'cheating on him' or the wife in Canada that her husband was enjoying himself with English girls. Sometimes, of course, these stories were true. By January 1943 the senior Protestant chaplain of the 1st Division (which, be it remembered, had been in England since 1939) was recommending furloughs in Canada for men with long service overseas, 'to arrest the disintegration of family life in Canada.' 'There is a limit to how much the human spirit can endure. The fidelity of many men and women, which has stood the test of more than three years separation, is showing signs of breaking.'[66] From the beginning, there were a few instances of

return to Canada on compassionate grounds, and in October 1941 a routine order provided a procedure; but by April 1943 only 112 cases had been approved for action. A larger number of officers and men went home as instructors or to take courses; 944 officers and 3750 men had had this good fortune by the end of July 1944. A slightly larger group were sent home as escorts for prisoners of war – a total of 4758 all ranks during the period 1941–4.[67] All this was a drop in the bucket.

The matter really came to a head in Italy, where the 1st Division was now serving. The chaplain of the Loyal Edmonton Regiment, Honorary Major E.J. Bailey, wrote an article in the *Eighth Army News* pointing out that other combatant countries had schemes for leave for long-service men and that the question was 'a matter of deep concern' to the Canadian soldier.[68] General Burns, commanding the 1st Corps in Italy, wrote to CMHQ in April 1944 emphasizing the seriousness of the problem as Canadians there saw it: 'Many of these men have been away from home for four years and, briefly, their feeling is that few homes can be expected to hold together when the husband has been away so long.'[69]

The Canadian authorities struggled with the problem, which was complicated by the shortage of infantry reinforcements in 1944. Finally, in November of that year, a plan was announced under which 450 men per month, having completed 'five years satisfactory continuous service overseas,' could be given leave to Canada. The first draft sailed at the end of November. Although the total number of men involved was small, there is no doubt that the mere existence of the scheme improved the morale of the Canadian Army Overseas in the final months of the war.[70] It may even have saved some marriages.

Canadian naval men serving in Britain were seldom there for extended periods and thus the problem of home leave did not arise. It did in the RCAF, however; and on 11 September 1943 it was announced that aircrew personnel who had completed one operational tour followed by a period of at least six months of instructional duty were eligible for a period of leave in Canada. As with the army, there were certain conditions attached: both suitably qualified replacements and sufficient shipping accommodation must be available. The plan was extended in July 1944 to include ground crew with three years' service overseas.[71] The air force thus got a rather better deal than the army.

No statistician will ever compute the number of Canadian servicemen overseas who were faithful to their Canadian wives in 1939–45, or the number of wives who were unshakably true to their absent husbands. But there were certainly many, just as there were many who failed to stand the gaff. One thing is sure; rank had nothing to do with it. In Canada, the Colonel's Lady and Judy O'Grady alike grappled with their private miseries and anxieties, while abroad the Colonel and Sergeant O'Grady confronted theirs. That some Canadian senior officers in England consoled themselves with English women was well known and sniggered at. An officer who was then a junior member of the staff at a Canadian headquarters has recalled – no names, no pack-drill – that his brigadier was absent almost every weekend, and that the junior alone knew the telephone number where he could be reached in emergency. It was far from a unique case. That particular distinguished officer's Canadian marriage is understood to have survived the liaison abroad; but another Canadian brigadier has frankly described in his memoirs how at the end of the war he divorced his Canadian wife in favour of a woman he had met overseas – in his case, not an English but a Dutch lady.[72]

As we have already said, the story told in this chapter is inevitably a mixture of darkness and light. It should end with a ray of sunshine on the page. Every Canadian serviceman who spent much time there has some reason to remember the women of Britain. Unflinchingly cheerful under the bombs, inventively hospitable in times when hospitality was very difficult, taking trouble to provide a touch of home for people whose own homes were on the other side of the world, it is not surprising that so many Canadians recall British women with affection and gratitude, or that so many of them returned to Canada with British brides.

CHAPTER SIX

The Seamy Side

IN CHAPTER 2 we described the problems that arose when the Canadians, in the beginning largely untrained and undisciplined, found themselves set down in England in a society that was strange to them and that also found them rather strange. Troubles were inevitable and sometimes serious. They grew less as the Canadians acquired discipline and as both parties became accustomed to the relationship. But troubles there always were.

We need to look at the legal machinery by which these problems were dealt with in the army. Of military offences, affecting only military personnel, we need say little. A serviceman charged with an offence against military regulations could be dealt with either summarily, by his commanding officer, if the offence was minor, or by court martial* if it was more serious or if the person charged demanded it. Civil offences, particularly where members of the civil population were involved, were a matter for the British civil courts.

Some people may be surprised to learn that the basic legislation governing the discipline of the Canadian Army during the Second World War was the Army Act enacted by the British parliament. This was by virtue of Section 69 of Canada's Militia Act, which provided, 'The *Army Act* for the time being in force in Great Britain, the King's regulations, and all other laws applicable to His Majesty's troops in Canada [this act went back to the days when British troops were still stationed in Canada] and not inconsistent with this Act or the regulations made hereunder, shall have force and effect as if they had been enacted by the Parliament of Canada for the government of the Militia.' Thus the Army Act was the law administered by Canadian Army courts martial and commanding officers, unless there was a Canadian law or regulation superseding some portion of it.

---

*A general court martial, normally consisting of not fewer than five officers presided over by an officer not below the rank of colonel, was required for the trial of an officer or of any person accused of a capital offence. Trials of other ranks for ordinary offences were conducted by field general courts martial, normally composed of a minimum of three officers presided over by a field officer, that is, an officer not below the rank of major; these courts in effect replaced the 'district court martial' of peacetime. Courts martial were advised on points of law by a legal officer called a judge advocate.

The relation between British and Canadian forces was governed by the 'Visiting Forces (British Commonwealth) Acts, 1933,' passed by the British and Canadian parliaments. These virtually identical acts were passed as a result of the Statute of Westminster, 1931, which established the effective legislative independence of Canada and the other dominions of the Commonwealth. They provided for two types of relationship between the two countries' forces: 'serving together' and 'in combination.' The latter was intended primarily for use in a theatre of operations, where a Canadian division or other formation might be acting under British command; it provided a legal basis for a British commander exercising operational command in such cases. 'Serving together,' the lawyers decided, applied to more peaceful circumstances such as those in the United Kingdom, where essentially the Canadian force was independent of British command. (Exceptions included the service of the 1st Canadian Corps in Sussex, where it was actually placed 'in combination' and under the operational direction of the general officer commanding-in-chief the British South Eastern Command.) 'Serving together,' however, was recognized as involving mutual acceptance of rank and powers of command between the two forces.[1] Thus, for example, the powers of the military police of each army were officially respected by the other. This did not mean that the policemen were liked; it is fair to say that the British 'redcaps' were universally unpopular with all ranks of the Canadian Army.

A point of importance is the fact that the Canadian forces fully accepted the powers and jurisdiction of British civil courts. Section 41 of the Army Act provided, 'a person subject to military law when in His Majesty's dominions may be tried by any competent civil court for any offence for which he would be triable if he were not subject to military law.' In view of the close integration of the Canadian and British services, it would have been difficult to follow any other plan; but it came naturally to the Canadians, since the British and Canadian judicial and legal systems were virtually identical, and Canadians had an inherited respect for British justice. Moreover, there was the precedent of the First World War, when the Canadians in the beginning were merely the troops of a self-governing colony, and no one thought of questioning the fact that they were subject to the jurisdiction of British courts.

The Americans, when they arrived in Britain in 1942, took a wholly dissimilar line. This was inevitable, for their history was quite different from the Canadians'. The merest suggestion of American soldiers being tried in British courts would have raised a political storm in the United States. As the result of American insistence, the British parliament quickly passed the United States of America (Visiting Forces) Act, accepting the principle that all offences of any sort committed by United States servicemen in the United Kingdom should be tried only in United States service courts.[2]

The Canadian practice resulted in many Canadians appearing in British civil courts. If a Canadian serviceman was picked up by the British civil or military police for an offence that could properly be called military, such as drunkenness, he was normally handed over to the Canadian military authorities to be dealt with. But if the offence was civil – such as breaking and entering, theft, rape, or murder – the offender found himself being tried by British process, and if found guilty suffering whatever penalty a British judge might impose. In fact, during the war six Canadian soldiers in the United Kingdom who were found guilty of murder were hanged by the judgment of British courts. In such cases the Canadian authorities took the responsibility of ensuring that the accused was properly defended and had every chance.[3] We shall see that in at least some of these cases the Canadian government made unsuccessful representations for clemency.

A British writer has pointed out that these legal arrangements had one very unfortunate consequence from the Canadian point of view. American offenders against Britons were tried by American courts martial, not open to the press. Canadians in similar cases were tried in civil courts, and the trials were fully and sometimes sensationally reported in the newspapers. It was the Canadians who got the bad publicity, and newspaper readers were likely to get the impression that they were responsible for far more crime than the Americans, though the latter were ultimately much more numerous in Britain.[4]

A British magistrate, faced with a Canadian soldier accused of a comparatively mild misdemeanour, often preferred to err on the side of leniency. Here, in effect, he would say, is a young man who has come across the sea to help us in our trouble; this is a case where severity would be out of place. This happened so frequently that Canadian officers became alarmed; leniency, they thought, could go too far, and would merely encourage the offender and his friends to feel that they could misbehave with the prospect of comparative immunity. In the interest of what the Army Act called 'good order and military discipline,' accordingly, they made various attempts to discourage the British courts from showing misplaced kindness to delinquent Canadians. In the autumn of 1940 two Canadians, convicted of robbery with violence, were merely bound over to keep the peace. Canadian Military Headquarters took the matter up with the high commissioner, suggesting that he raise the general question of undue leniency with Herbert Morrison, the home secretary. Massey's diary records that he spoke to Morrison on the subject, but says nothing about Morrison's reaction, which suggests that he may have been non-committal.[5]

The problem continued to vex Canadian commanders, and in July 1942 General Crerar, commanding the Canadian Corps in Sussex, wrote about it to Sir James Cassels and Rowland Burrows, chairmen, respectively, of the East and West Sussex Quarter Sessions, and to the county clerks of the peace. He said, 'this tendency to admonish, or "bind over," rather than award a real punishment to match an evident crime, is quite contrary to what the very great majority of all ranks in the Canadian Corps would really desire to see happen. The good name of Canada means a very great deal more to all than does soft treatment of an undeserving individual.'[6] The curious thing is that no record has been found of a reply to this letter. It seems possible that the British magistrates resented what they may have considered improper interference with the performance of their judicial functions, and found it easier to maintain silence than to give Crerar an answer which he in turn might have resented.

What is probably a glimpse of the real feelings of the British authorities in this matter appears in Massey's diary for 1945.

On 31 January, he records, he saw the home secretary at the latter's request: 'Morrison is very much disturbed over our recent intervention on behalf of ... [a Canadian soldier] ... whose execution was postponed at our request, as it turned out for no sufficient reason. It is quite clear that in making representations on behalf of practically all Canadians convicted of murder, whether [we] have a good case or not, we are using up all our credit. Ottawa should show some discretion in nipping in the bud appeals that are not merited. Morrison feels very strongly about the matter and indeed doubts the moral right of one government to intervene in the process of justice under another, although he agrees that it is natural that we should ask for clemency when we really feel that there are grounds for such a request.' When one considers that Canada was an independent country of the Commonwealth, the situation seems a trifle strange. Occasionally the suggestion was made that it would have been more satisfactory if, like the United States, she had handled all her own disciplinary problems in the United Kingdom through Canadian courts martial; but it would have been extremely difficult to introduce such a system in the middle of the war.

One could spend hundreds of pages describing what General Montague once called 'our worrisome disciplinary troubles.'[7] In any environment, several hundred thousand servicemen would be bound to create a great variety of problems. They ranged from major crime, including murder, to the innumerable petty misdemeanours that took up the time of Canadian commanding officers and British magistrates.

We have spoken of the Canadians' introduction to the institution of the British public house, and its consequences in the form of chronic drunkenness. More than anything else, this is the offence that critics of the Canadians dwell on in the early years. Vincent Massey recorded an interview with 'Major Nicholson, Chief Constable of Surrey' in 1941:[8] 'He said the Canadian Soldiers were no more troublesome than U.K. troops. Their offences were different–chiefly due to drink.' Brigadier C.A.P. Murison, the senior administrative officer of the 7th (shortly the Canadian) Corps, talked to Nicholson in December 1940 and set down his testimony in more detail: 'He stated that over a period of approximately 12 months, 221 offences had been undoubtedly committed by Canadian Soldiers, but that proof sufficient to obtain the conviction of individuals had only been established in 63 cases. He added that in only two particulars did he consider that the Canadian Soldiers compared unfavourably with British, namely, drunkenness and speeding. He said that in his opinion the more serious offences in which Canadian Soldiers had been involved could, in nearly every case, be put down to drunkenness.'[9] There had been particular trouble, Nicholson said, at Witley Camp, where there had been bad Canadian riots at the end of the last war which were still remembered.[10] Here there had been 'a recent manslaughter case in which a Canadian Soldier had killed a civilian in a brawl.'

It was common knowledge that pub brawls involving Canadians most frequently took place on pay nights, when the soldier had money to buy drink. The troops were paid semi-monthly, and in October 1940 the suggestion was made that weekly payment should be substituted, with a view to reducing rowdy conduct on pay nights. McNaughton and

Montague strongly recommended this policy but, after long discussion, Ottawa in its wisdom rejected it. More frequent payments in Canada were not considered necessary and the minister of national defence, Colonel Ralston, took the view that additional pay days in Britain would unnecessarily complicate the pay system.[11] The decision seems short-sighted.

The fact nevertheless remains that with the passage of time drink became a less serious problem. Canadians came to think of a pub as a place to enjoy oneself, not a place to get drunk. Increasingly they became welcome guests. In the summer of 1941 the *Brighton and Hove Herald* reported that the men of the 2nd Field Regiment RCA had presented a brass plaque to a pub near Brighton 'in appreciation of hospitality received.' The paper commented, 'Is mine host proud of that tablet? I should say he is. "They were just grand guys," he said. "I have had other units in the district; they are all good boys, but somehow they don't think of these things like the Canucks do. I suppose the Canucks are a long way from home and they appreciate a little kindness."'[12] That pub was not unique. Back of CMHQ in London there was an establishment called the Horse and Dolphin whose bar bore in due course a long line of small brass plates with the names of Canadians who had found the place a pleasant retreat.*

There is statistical support for the decline of drunkenness. In September 1942 CMHQ prepared for the first time a general

'Report on Discipline of the Canadian Army Overseas.'[13] The covering letter summarizing its contents ran in part as follows, with reference particularly to military offences:

The most prevalent offence is absence without leave. It accounts for rather better than 50% of the total.

The next most prevalent class of offence is that coming within the Army Act Section 40 – conduct or neglect to the prejudice of good order and military discipline. Roughly one third of the total number of offences are of this class.

The third most prevalent offence is that of drunkenness which accounts for a remarkably small percentage of the whole.*

A similar general report submitted in March 1943[14] remarked, 'A.W.L. [absence without leave] has remained the most prevalent offence, drunkenness is still a very small proportion of the whole.' A third (and last) such report, prepared in June 1943, noted, 'Drunkenness does not appear to be a very serious factor.'[15] These statements would have surprised officers in 1940. Perhaps one should not overstate their significance, for it seems likely that drunkenness had something to do with at least some of the charges laid under Section 40, but at the lowest valuation they are striking.

As for offences dealt with by civil courts, the report of September 1942 remarked,

---

*Two articles by Joyce Hibbert, in *Legion* magazine for December 1982 and March 1984, describe various small memorials of the Canadian 'occupation' that survive in England.

*This report dealt with the whole period from the first arrival of Canadian troops in Britain until the end of August 1942; but the information was complete and thoroughly reliable only for the latter part of the period.

(a) The most prevalent offences ... are those involving theft, larceny and burglary and the next most prevalent are those involving assault.

(b) A total of 923 soldiers have been convicted by the civil courts during the period under review [December 1939 through August 1942]. This figure is not entirely accurate by reason of the fact that the records for the early stages are not complete but are sufficiently accurate to show that the proportion of the troops involved in civil prosecutions is relatively small.

We have to note that the figures given are those of convictions, not charges; and we have seen the tendency of British courts to treat Canadians with what Canadian authorities thought undue leniency. The available statistics fully support the generalization of the CMHQ report of June 1943: 'As an average figure, 4 to 5 soldiers out of every 10,000 are involved with the civil authorities each month.' It would have been more accurate to say, 'involved with the civil authorities to the point of conviction.'[16] It was regrettable that these crimes, largely committed against the people of the United Kingdom, should have taken place at all; but some satisfaction could be felt in the fact that they were so comparatively few in number.

Officers as well as 'other ranks' got into trouble, though usually in different ways. The CMHQ report on discipline covering the period through August 1942 had this to say on general courts martial – in effect, trials of officers:

During the period in question there have been 71 officers tried by General Court Martial. Of these 6 have been cashiered and 21 dismissed the Service.* The total represents less than 1% of the number of officers in the U.K. at the present time and in a few cases officers have been tried on more than one occasion.

The great majority of the offences come within Section 40 of the Army Act. A large number of these had to do with the careless handling of the officer's bank account and the consequent non-payment of cheques.

Drunkenness and absence without leave account for most of the remaining offences.

It was not only other ranks who came to grief through alcohol.

Inevitably, Canadian misbehaviour was resented by the people who suffered by it, and almost equally inevitably the resentment was reflected in the press. We have said that the winter of 1941–2 was a particularly bad period for Canadian Army morale, and therefore one when the misbehaviour was particularly in evidence. An incident in January got into the newspapers back in Canada. An anonymous letter in the *Sussex Daily News* accused Canadian soldiers of 'hooliganism' and added, 'unless the officers in charge of these brutes can control them it would be a good thing for the authorities to apply for their removal.' This suggestion drew a stinging reply in the same paper from Earl Winterton, MP. Winterton, who had fought in Arabia with T.E. Lawrence, said he wrote as 'Senior Member of Parliament in length of service for Sussex and as a former Cabinet Minister anxious to support a maximum war effort for the whole Empire; as one who knows Canada, and

*Cashiering was defined as a more ignominious form of dismissal.

has been brought into intimate relationship with the Canadian forces in England.' He called the correspondent's remark a 'monstrous thing for any person, especially one writing under the cloak of anonymity, to say about servicemen and fellow-subjects from another part of the Empire here to defend us from invasion.' Not denying that there were offences committed by Canadians, he said these were the work of a minority. Moreover, he continued, 'In my constituency some eighteen months ago the most serious wilful damage done to property was by a certain unit of the British Army. Neither my constituents nor I thought it patriotic or desirable to write to the press about it.'[17]

We have said that British magistrates tended to show what some considered undue leniency in dealing with Canadian offenders. There were also magistrates who used hard words about Canadians generally when faced with a Canadian in the dock. In this same January of 1942 the sensational London newspaper *News of the World*, which had itself given Canadians some poor publicity in its time, lashed out at these abusive members of the bench. It pointed out the 'galling situation' in which the Canadians found themselves in England, 'forced by circumstances beyond their control to remain in comparative idleness' while troops of other Commonwealth countries fought the enemy; it was not surprising in these circumstances that Canadians should sometimes turn up in court. The paper went on:

For these reasons we deplore the attitude of some of our police-court magistrates before whom Canadian soldiers have appeared from time to time.

Observations reflecting on the conduct and behaviour of the Canadian soldiers as a whole have been made – and reported in the Press – by justices of the peace who ought to have known better.

Comments like 'What, the Canadians *again*?' and 'A discredit to the Canadian Army' have become almost stock phrases.

In our view this attitude is both unfair and unjustifiable.

With millions of men under arms, the editorial went on, it was inevitable that servicemen should be involved in a large proportion of the cases before the courts. 'But no magistrate is sufficiently tactless in these circumstances to remark "What, the British Army again?" or the Royal Navy, or the Royal Air Force, as the case may be.' Why, then, single out the Canadians? 'May we venture to hope that magistrates in future will temper with discretion and fair words any observations they may be tempted to make when a "black sheep" of this magnificent army from the Dominion stands in their police-court dock.'[18]

In May 1943 a complaint against the Canadians in Sussex came in from a distant and unlikely quarter. Lieutenant-General Sir Henry Pownall was commander-in-chief Persia-Iraq, a dull and inactive appointment. This perhaps contributed to his writing to the adjutant general at the War Office, General Sir Ronald Adam, about events in Sussex. He had had a letter from the commanding officer of a battalion with many Sussex men in its ranks reporting his men's alarm at what they heard from their home county. The colonel wrote in part:

Local papers received from Sussex are full of reports of court cases of Canadian soldiers' misbehaviour, assaulting women, etc. A local paper reported a speech by the Mayor of Brighton to the effect that 7,000 Sussex girls had married Canadians ...Men, in letters, are hearing of members of their own and other families bearing illegitimate children by Canadian soldiers. At least one N.C.O. of this Unit has heard that his wife is expecting a child, although he has been abroad for a year. A Canadian is suspected to be the father ...

Men cannot be expected to do themselves or their Units justice if their minds are not easy about their families and homes. There is more bitter feeling against the Canadians at present than against the Germans.

Adam, who was on first-name terms with General McNaughton, was naturally disturbed by this unpleasant epistle. Before forwarding it to McNaughton he asked his deputy assistant director of public relations to have a look at recent Sussex newspapers. The DADPR reported that he had read the files of half a dozen papers, and 'The number of Police Court cases in which Canadian soldiers were concerned was extremely small.' After detailing a number of actual reports he concluded, 'Some months ago it was very common to see six or seven reports in a single paper of police court cases in which Canadian soldiers were defendants. From the above report it will be appreciated that there has been a great falling off of any publicity of this character.'

McNaughton replied to Adam giving a few solid facts: 'It is unfortunately true that up until some 6 months ago the British press played up spectacularly any court cases affecting Canadians. In the Counties of Sussex and Surrey, during the six months ending 5 Jul 43, 297 Canadian soldiers were convicted of civil offences. This is equivalent to 1 offender per 12,000 troops per week. These cases were principally minor ones such as drunkenness, petty theft, etc. Offences against women totalled 15 – or 1 per 200,000 men per week.' McNaughton declined to regard as tragic the fact that Canadian soldiers were marrying British girls. He mentioned the precautions taken to ensure against over-hasty marriages. Sussex men, he remarked, 'surely must realize that the problem is universal and applies as well to the Canadian away from home. Men from all parts of the Empire go to Canada under the Air Training Scheme and many of them marry Canadian girls.' As for illegitimate children, the only relevant information available was that during the nine months ending 1 July 1943 there were 101 maintenance orders issued for the entire Canadian Army Overseas. The Canadian general remarked a trifle acidly, 'It takes two people to produce an illegitimate child, and illegitimate children were being born in Sussex before the arrival of Canadian troops.'

McNaughton went on to say that he considered the Canadian soldier had behaved, and was still behaving, well, under rather difficult conditions. He had entered into the life of the communities where he was stationed, 'and there has been formed a very real bond between the people of Sussex and the Canadian troops.' McNaughton said that he understood Pownall's problem, for Canadian soldiers too received letters alleging infidelities and other matters of family concern; arrangements had been made for investigating such cases, and the reports were often found to be inaccurate and perhaps malicious.[19]

Some time later, additional statistics having been received from the civil police, it was computed that in Sussex during the first six months of 1943 the average number of offences against women per 10,000 troops was 7 by British troops and 3.22 by Canadians. A letter to Adam to this effect was prepared for McNaughton's signature, but with characteristic good sense he refrained from sending it; there was no point, he thought, in making what might seem invidious comparisons.[20]

It's only fair to say that the newspapers sometimes had tragic and unpleasant stories about Canadians to report from Sussex. Perhaps the most sensational was that of a murder that happened at Portslade, near Brighton, in March 1943.* The murderer was a twenty-five-year-old Canadian soldier, the victim, an Englishwoman whose husband was a prisoner in Germany. The Canadian, who said he was deeply in love with the woman, discovered that she had another lover, also a Canadian. He shot her dead with a Bren gun (incidentally stolen from the Home Guard), wounding his rival at the same time. The woman had been pregnant. When the culprit was first tried the jury failed to agree. In a second trial he was found guilty of murder. His appeal failed, and he was one of the six Canadians who were hanged.[21]

It should also be said that Pownall's men from Sussex were not alone in their worries. Noël Coward, visiting the Middle East to entertain the troops in this same year 1943, found British servicemen troubled by reports of Canadians and Americans in Britain spending money freely and getting too friendly with their sweethearts and wives. He thought, undoubtedly truly, that these stories were encouraged by enemy propaganda as well as by irresponsible letters from home, and tried to reassure the men he talked to by telling them that the vast majority of the American and dominion visitors whom he encountered were thoroughly well-behaved.[22]

'Petty theft' is a phrase that frequently gets into the records, and sometimes into the correspondence of generals. In June 1942 General Montgomery wrote to General Crerar complaining of thefts by Canadian troops during the recent exercise 'Tiger.' Police reports, he said, referred 'chiefly to thefts of poultry, fowls, etc.,' but there was mention too of 'money, cigarettes, tea and so on.' He remarked that he got more complaints of this sort about the Canadians than from the area of the 12th British Corps, which was also under his command. Crerar said in reply that the problem chiefly arose during exercises when troops were away from their normal stations; even so, the ratio of one civilian claim, or a little more, per 1000 troops in four months did not depress him unduly. He added, 'As regards the attitude of the Police, Superintendent Catt, my P.L.O. [police liaison officer], stated this week that, with the exception of some chicken stealing during "TIGER" there was no problem of petty theft amongst troops in the Canadian Corps District at present, and at a Police conference on the 18th of June ... the Chief Constables of both East and West Sussex both stated they were not disturbed as to civilian offences by Canadians.'[23] Nevertheless, Crerar proceeded to issue to his corps a strong letter on the subject of petty crime, poultry being especially mentioned.[24]

---

*For an account of another case, the Hankley Common murder, from Surrey, not Sussex, see Tom Tullett, *Strictly Murder: Famous Cases of Scotland Yard's Murder Squad* (London 1979), 158–67.

It is just possible that Monty tended to overemphasize crime among Canadians; but there is evidence from the culprits themselves that some Canadians did not regard chicken-stealing as a particularly serious offence. The postal censors noted a letter written after manoeuvres in the autumn of 1941 by a soldier of the Saskatoon Light Infantry: 'The English soldiers lived on hard tack, but that wouldn't do for Canadians, especially when the farmers go to bed so early and cannot take their orchards and chickens with them ... so I and my mates lived like kings.'[25] The owners of the fruit and chickens would take a very different view. No doubt they made claims and were reimbursed.

On one occasion Canadian chicken-stealing was brought rather forcibly to the attention of the Canadian high commissioner. In December 1941 Mr and Mrs Massey were visiting Lord and Lady Moyne at their house in West Sussex. This is Massey's account: 'At dinner we ate two chickens which had been purloined by Canadian Soldiers from the Moynes' poultry-house, traced to their billet by a trail of white feathers, followed by the two girls and returned by the officer's order plucked, cleaned & dressed, to be eaten in part by a Canadian (V.M.)!'[26] This was evidently one case of chicken-stealing that never came before a British court.

By a curious chance an eminent British naval officer caught an intimate glimpse of Canadian chicken-stealing proclivities. Captain (later Vice-Admiral) John Hughes Hallett, the chief naval planner at Combined Operations Headquarters, had the original idea during training for the Dieppe raid of getting himself attached to a Canadian infantry unit, disguised as a private soldier, in order to find out what combined operations looked like to the troops. As 'Private Charles Hallett' he got himself into the Queen's Own Cameron Highlanders of Canada and spent some time with them. (The first plan was that he should accompany them on the raid; but when the operation was revived after being cancelled he found himself naval force commander.) The Canadians, he recorded, were a nice bunch of chaps, but a little short on conversation. Incidentally, when Mr Churchill asked his opinion of them, he assured the British prime minister that they would 'fight like hell.' But our present concern is with chickens. Describing the Camerons' daily routine, Hughes Hallett wrote, 'about 9 p.m. we had an unofficial meal which the Canadians called "lunch," and which normally consisted of one or two chickens stolen from a local farm and boiled in milk. After that we went to bed and slept the sleep of the just.'[27]

Chicken-stealing was not unknown in the RCAF, but lacking the army's experience gained in field exercises the airmen got smaller dividends from it. J. Douglas Harvey of 408 Squadron RCAF describes raids on 'chicken farms' which turned out badly because chickens cooked over open fires were unpalatable.[28] Hughes Hallett's friends in the Camerons could have told 408 a thing or two.

As McNaughton remarked to General Adam, there were times when the Canadians were getting a bad press. The reader may remember Lord Winterton's remark that misbehaviour by British soldiers seemed to get less attention. On several occasions Canadian authorities tried to bring influence to bear to reduce the number of adverse references. It was a ticklish matter, for press freedom was involved and, after all, no one could deny that there were offences committed by Canadians. The question was, were these offences getting undue publicity? Some progress was made. The public relations officer at CMHQ reported in November 1942 that thirteen letters had been written to newspapers that had 'given prominence to the Canadian angle in crime stories,' and that all of them had promised some degree of co-operation in playing down this angle in future. In December the PRO wrote to the *News of the World*, whose editor replied that he had given instructions that, in future, Canadian defendants in court should be referred to not as Canadians 'but merely as "soldiers."' We have already seen this highly sensational paper exerting itself to create good-will towards the men from Canada. The British Broadcasting Corporation was prevailed upon to alter a radio play in which a character had been advertised as a 'well lit-up Canadian soldier in the last train home'; he became an English soldier.[29] Nobody, apparently, took exception to the idea of an Englishman being soused in public.

Obviously, the propriety of this sort of action in defence of the Canadian 'image' could be argued about indefinitely. But there is not much doubt that at times the Canadians had been getting rather less than a fair shake from the British media.

Once convicted, how were offenders punished? Apart from the numerous lesser penalties prescribed in the Army Act or other British statutes, a Canadian officer or soldier might be sentenced by a Canadian court martial or a British civil court to a period of imprisonment or of penal servitude, the latter involving hard labour. An officer sentenced to either of these punishments was automatically cashiered. These sentences were normally served in a British civil prison. A soldier (but not an officer) might be sentenced to a period of detention, to be served in a detention barracks or other form of military custody, but not in a civil prison. The death penalty was still in effect for murder under civil law, and under the Army Act for treachery or mutiny; no longer, as it had been in the First World War, for desertion or cowardice. This humane reform, which also applied to the air force, was effected by an amendment to the Army Act passed in 1930 under Ramsay MacDonald's second Labour government.[30]

In the earliest days of the Canadian sojourn in England, Canadian soldiers sentenced to detention usually served the sentence in the British Army's detention barracks in Aldershot, the famous 'glasshouse.' In the summer of 1940, however, after the Dunkirk evacuation, it became difficult to find accommodation for Canadian offenders; the War Office explained that there was a shortage 'due to the unexpected return of the B.E.F. from France.'[31] The ultimate answer was to set up a Canadian Army detention barracks. In requesting authority for a war establishment for this unit, CMHQ explained to Ottawa that there were 'comparatively large numbers approx 400 soldiers incorrigible bad characters in Holding Units' (the units in the Aldershot area holding reinforcements) and no effective means of detaining them.[32] The new barracks was temporarily located at Witley, Surrey; in April 1942 it was moved to a permanent location at Headley Down, Hampshire. By the middle of 1943 there were 650 soldiers in custody at the establishment. It was not, of course, used merely as a convenient place to hold 'incorrigible bad characters'; every man committed to it had been sentenced for a specific offence. Soon after the move to Headley the deputy provost marshal at CMHQ wrote, 'The system of training at the Canadian Detention Barracks as compared with the British Detention Barracks varies somewhat, in that at the Canadian Detention Barracks more time is spent on teaching long term s.u.s. [Soldiers under Sentence] to learn some useful trade which will not only make them better soldiers but also better citizens. The Educational Department are cooperating and at present several s.u.s. who are illiterate are being taught to read and write.' Classes were being held in tailoring, carpentry, shoe repairing, and first aid. As soon as equipment arrived there would be instruction in automotive engineering and welding.[33]

In 1943, at the request of the RCAF, it was agreed that men of that service sentenced to detention might serve their time in the Canadian Army Detention Barracks. It was explained that 'only personnel of the London Headquarters of the R.C.A.F.' would be involved.[34] The fact was that this was the only establishment actually commanded by the 'Air Officer Commanding-in-Chief, R.C.A.F. Overseas Headquarters.' Other offending Canadian airmen, whether in RAF or RCAF units, would serve their sentences in Royal Air Force detention barracks.

The Detention Barracks population tended to increase; and as the end of the war in Europe approached the Canadian authorities looked about for additional accommodation. It appeared that Reading Gaol – famous in English literature for its association with Oscar Wilde – might be available; and on 9 April 1945 the home secretary informed the Canadian high commissioner that Canada could have the place as a detention barracks at least temporarily.[35] This was timely; for next month the inmates at Headley celebrated VE-Day – the day of Victory in Europe – with a riot and a mass escape. A large force of Canadian troops then surrounded the barracks to prevent further trouble, and 370 inmates were transferred to the greater security of Reading.[36] Somewhat exaggerated accounts of the affair appeared in British newspapers. On 28 June the Canadian Army paper *The Maple Leaf* quoted the London *Evening News* as saying, 'Of the 100 prisoners who made a mass break-out from the Canadian military prison near Aldershot on VE-night 13 are still at large.' The actual facts, *The Maple Leaf* accurately said, were that only sixty men had broken out and only seven were still at large. The *News* had also asserted that 'Hundreds of deserters and absentees from the Canadian Army are on the run' in England. Here again *The Maple Leaf* gave the facts: 239 men classed as deserters in Britain out of 370,000 Canadian soldiers who had come to the country.[37]

Apart from security, Reading had little to commend it. It had not been used as a prison since 1919; it was still lighted by gas, and sanitary arrangements were extremely primitive. The Canadian staff set to work to improve things. But for all its shortcomings, in the conditions of 1945 the place was badly needed. From July to November 1945 another Canadian detention barracks was in operation at Alton, Hampshire.[38]

Canadians sentenced to imprisonment were incarcerated in British civil prisons ('His Majesty's Prisons'). Precise statistics of their number seem impossible to come by. A not wholly satisfactory compilation by the Canadian Provost Corps extending from the beginning of 1943 to the end of February 1946 indicates a total in the vicinity of 1640: again, not a large number when one considers how many Canadian soldiers were in the country. These figures do not include the Royal Canadian Air Force or the Royal Canadian Navy, which also contributed to the prison population. Moreover, it is clear that the total includes some men sentenced for military offences on the Continent during the fighting there. After the Normandy D-Day, convictions for desertion, and a smaller number for cowardice, begin to appear; the normal sentence in these cases is three years' penal servitude. In the earlier war some of these men would almost certainly have been shot.

Except for these military offences, the list of crimes is very much the same as the prison records would show in peacetime. There are a few cases of murder, in which the supreme penalty had not been exacted and imprisonment was substituted. There are a certain number of cases of manslaughter. There are a great many convictions for larceny or theft, and a good many for assault, including rape. There are a few cases of buggery, and a few of bigamy. There are some short sentences for dangerous driving. All told, it is a sordid record, but one that could be paralleled in any large community, civil or military, in peace or war.

It would be pleasant if one could record that the half-million Canadians who found themselves dwelling in the United Kingdom in 1939–45 were universally well-behaved and moral people. Humanity being what it is, that was not the case. The vast majority of Canadian service people gave their British hosts no cause for complaint. That some made trouble was often the result of youth and high spirits, a new and strange environment, and the social disruptions of wartime. And – let's face it – it would have been contrary to all experience if in so large a body there had not been some actual criminal element that found opportunities in these war conditions and had to be dealt with as such elements have to be in all societies. Happily, such characters were a small proportion of the half-million; and the record as a whole can be looked back upon with a considerable degree of satisfaction.

CHAPTER SEVEN

Six Years of It

ON 30 APRIL 1945 Adolf Hitler, besieged by the Russians in his bunker in Berlin, shot himself. On 4 May the Germans on Field-Marshal Montgomery's front in Northwest Europe surrendered to the British commander. The following day hostilities in that area ceased, and for the soldiers of Britain and Canada the war with Germany was over.

From that moment, inevitably, Canadians overseas, whether on the Continent or in Britain, thought mainly of their own futures. For the soldier there were three main possibilities: service (which was to be on a purely voluntary basis) in the Canadian Army Pacific Force which was to take part in the war still continuing against Japan; service (either voluntary or otherwise) in the Canadian Army Occupation Force which was to play a part, for a time, in the occupation of Germany; or return to Canada for demobilization. So far as possible, the army tried to apply the rule 'first in, first out,' and a point system was instituted which gave preference for repatriation to men with the longest service. The necessity of maintaining the force as a going concern, however, meant that officers and

men doing important jobs had to be retained in some cases beyond the time when their points might have entitled them to release.[1]

As soon as possible after the cease-fire, all the Canadian troops in Germany, with the exception of those intended for the Occupation Force, were moved into the Netherlands, where they spent the months until they could be repatriated. In the meantime, leaves to Britain were available for the many men who desired them. Repatriation was by way of England, where the Canadian Reinforcement Units in the Aldershot area became Repatriation Depots with the task of organizing the homeward movement. Although Canada had no control of shipping, and at one time it was feared that there would be serious delays, that movement proceeded with satisfactory rapidity. During the second half of 1945 about 192,000 Canadian Army and RCAF personnel were sent off to Canada.[2] On VE-Day, 8 May 1945, there were 281,757 all ranks of the Canadian Army in Britain and on the Continent. Between then and the end of the year, 184,054 of them left for Canada. By 31 March 1946 there were only 17,745 army personnel left in the United Kingdom; on the Continent there were fewer than 800 apart from the Occupation Force. Later that year the Occupation Force itself was withdrawn, and by the end of January 1947 the strength of Canada's overseas army was down to 630 all ranks. In April of that year Canadian Military Headquarters, London, changed over to peacetime status as the Canadian Army Liaison Establishment; this symbolized the end of a remarkable chapter in the relations of Britain and Canada.[3]

One is constantly driven to compare the experience of 1939–45 with that of 1914–18. In the First World War the Canadians' final months in England were disturbed and turbulent. Almost inevitably, the machinery of repatriation and demobilization did not move as rapidly as the troops considered desirable. Some planned sailings had to be cancelled; some men were given special priority for compassionate reasons, which were not generally understood; some short-service men were sent back ahead of their normal times, simply to take advantage of shipping that suddenly became available; and these matters were not adequately explained to the troops at large. The result, perhaps not unnatural in the circumstances but certainly highly regrettable, was serious disorders. The official history records, 'In all, between November 1918 and June 1919, there were thirteen instances of riots or disturbances involving Canadian troops in England.'[4]

The worst of these was at Kinmel Park near Rhyl in North Wales, in March 1919. Over 17,000 Canadians had been collected here, growing angrier and angrier as shipping to take them home failed to materialize. A serious riot broke out, and

before it was quelled five soldiers were dead and some twenty-five wounded. The truth was bad enough, but grossly exaggerated accounts of the affair were printed in the British press. (The best story, perhaps, was that of the major with the Victoria Cross who had been trampled to death.) Later there was trouble in the south, notably at the big Canadian camp at Witley in Surrey, where many buildings were burned on 14 and 15 June. And the worst tragedy was at Epsom on 17 June; a riot started when a Canadian soldier and his wife were hustled by a crowd, and before it ended an elderly police sergeant was mortally hurt and seven other policemen injured.[5] Although the Canadians did not lack defenders among the British press, public, and judges, the events of 1919 did Canada's name no good in Britain, and we have seen that the memory of them lingered and was thrown up against a new generation of Canadians, who knew nothing about them, in the second war (above, pages 77 and 159).

The years 1945 and 1946 saw no repetition of the unpleasant happenings of 1919. There was, it is true, one thoroughly disgraceful episode: the Aldershot riots of 4 and 5 July 1945. Shops were looted and much damage done; by 31 March 1946 Canada had paid $41,541 to the victims. The perpetrators were severely dealt with; six men were convicted by courts martial, receiving sentences of from sixteen months to (in one case) seven years. Three of them, it is interesting to note, were members of the Pacific Force, the group enjoying the highest priority for repatriation (and repatriation was going forward rapidly at the time of the riots). General Montague wrote that Pacific Force men seemed to be the

'Now that the war is over we'll be soon leaving for Uncle Herbie's big ranch in Toronto!'

Some Canadian servicemen, like Herbie in this Bing Coughlin cartoon, were not quite accurate in describing their status in Canada to British wives and sweethearts.
(Reproduced by permission Director Information Services, DND)

ringleaders, men 'whom I cannot describe otherwise than as racketeers.'[6] (It was common talk that men were volunteering for the Pacific merely as a way of getting a quick trip back to Canada. There was a good chance that, as actually happened, the Japanese war would end and the Pacific Force would never fight; failing that, there was always desertion.)

Aldershot had never been a popular station with the Canadians. Nevertheless, the rioting of 1945 was almost universally condemned by all ranks of the Canadian Army. The evidence is the reports of the censors who were reading their letters. They quoted many writers, and the tone was generally one of total disgust. Soldiers on the Continent made particularly scathing comments. One private wrote, 'It was an awful dirty mean trick and it is only making the English people hate the Canadians. Our Army was loved by the English by their work over here. Some of them will get it. I think they should get 20 years.' Another private made a remark that many of his mates might have echoed: 'it's given us a damned bad name and besides it didn't get them anywhere, it would have been allright if they'd burned the Barracks down but instead they took their spite out on honest Shopkeepers. Everyone of these guys should get at least five years don't you think?'[7] It is pleasant to recall that the people of Aldershot forgave if not forgot; on 26 September 1945 they conferred the freedom of the borough on the Canadian Army Overseas.[8]

Certainly there are some kind words on record that are in striking contrast with 1919. An English mother wrote to Superior Camp (Ludshott, Hants) in January 1946 after what was probably the last of many Canadian Christmas parties for the children of the district. Her children hadn't been able to get to the party, but toys came for them anyway: 'The kindness of all Canadians to the little ones is something to be remembered forever. My experience is that they cannot see a child without going down the pocket for a chocolate bar or a stick of gum, or failing either a pat on the head ... God Bless Canada.'9 And in the following July Mrs M. Ironside and ninety-three other inhabitants of Thursley, near Witley, sent a letter to General Montague at CMHQ:

Since hearing lately of episodes in a nearby town [clearly Aldershot] I have been approached by several people in this village with the idea of finding some way of showing our appreciation of the excellent discipline and understanding with which Col. [Louis] Keene and his staff have run ... No 1 Canadian Repatriation Depot.

We have all enjoyed having the Canadians with us. Knowing the exuberance of spirits found in troops on their way home, we have frequently marvelled at the orderly behaviour of our local soldiers. This we know is due a great deal to the way they are handled and so wish to express our thanks.10

And here are some 'Remarks addressed from the Bench by W.H. Pilcher, Esq., J.P., Chairman of the Godalming [Surrey] Borough Petty Sessions':

As it is probably the last Annual Licensing Meeting before the departure of our Canadian soldier friends, I think a word of commendation is due to them and the troops generally. Although in the Court we do not see the best of them, looking beyond the range of a Magistrate's Court the Justices feel that the average standard of behaviour of the troops has been very good, especially in the streets at night. Even those who live on the main road have suffered very little disturbance and we all hope that this will be maintained during the difficult period of waiting for repatriation.

I should like the Superintendent to bring this expression to the notice of the Officer Commanding Witley Camp. Some share of the credit is due to the [liquor] Licensees and to the Police and we hope Godalming will preserve its good name in the matter.

Superintendent R. Webb endorsed entirely the remarks with regard to the behaviour of the troops, to which the Chairman replied, 'Great credit is due to you personally.'11

This was on 7 February 1946. It is worth recalling that Superintendent Webb himself had written to Brigadier T.J. Rutherford, commanding E Group of the Canadian Reinforcement Units, expressing appreciation of the 'excellent conduct' of Canadians during the local celebrations of VE-Day. Not one complaint had been received, which Webb thought evidence that the Canadians intended to retain 'that happy relation which has always existed between the Police and public of this district and their Canadian friends at Witley Camp.'12

In these communications it is possible to detect an undertone. It seems evident that the Justices, the police, and the good folk of Thursley had not wholly forgotten the nasty Witley riot of 1919 and, presumably, the troubles of 1940 (above, page 159). The Thursley people are praising not only 'our local soldiers' but also the intelligent administration that has kept them in line. One senses that the district may have

Clearing up the debris in Aldershot left by the rioting by some Canadian
soldiers awaiting repatriation, July 1945. (H.D. Robinson, PAC / DND, PA 147117)

regarded Witley Camp, with its turbulent past, as something of a ticking bomb. But in 1945–6 the bomb did not go off.

Not all the Canadians who had survived the war chose to go home. This was a repetition of 1918, when – in spite of official attempts to discourage men from taking discharge in England – some 22,000 Canadian soldiers did just that. It is worth remembering that only about 51 per cent of the Canadian Expeditionary Force of the first war were Canadian-born, and the vast majority of the rest were British, products of the great prewar immigration.[13] Therefore, many of the 22,000 were doubtless men who simply decided to remain in their native country. In the second war it was a standing joke that the ambition of every good Canadian soldier was to own an English pub. How many achieved it then there is no way of telling; but the same aspiration seems to have been present in the earlier generation, for one of the authors of this book, visiting Salisbury Plain in 1941, put up for the night in a modest pub run by a Canadian soldier of the old war whose wife and partner was a Frenchwoman. The number of Canadians who 'stayed on' in 1946 was smaller, related, no doubt, to the fact that the proportion of Canadian-born in the army of the second war was about 85 per cent. Again there was official discouragement – the pamphlet written to explain the army repatriation process to the troops said, 'Only in most exceptional circumstances, involving serious hardship, will soldiers be discharged outside of Canada.'[14] This led to complaints, and discharge boards were instructed to show some leniency in interpreting the 'hardship' clause.[15] In fact, however, the best figures available indicate that in all three services the number of Canadians discharged in the United Kingdom through December 1946 was only 5818. The total for the army was 3506 males and 107 members of the Canadian Women's Army Corps.[16] Some individuals doubtless found their own way back later, but for this there are no statistics. Much larger was the movement of new citizens towards Canada; as we have seen (above, page 141), over 61,000 war brides and children made the journey, and the vast majority of them came from Britain.

The most remarkable feature of the Canadian experience in Britain in the Second World War was the transformation of the Canadian soldier's relationship with the British people. In the beginning the relationship could not have been much worse; in the cold winter of 1939–40 in Aldershot the untrained and undisciplined men of the 1st Canadian Division disliked everything about the town and the country: the frigid barracks, the weather, the food, the strange and reserved people. And the unlicked Canadians' behaviour was far from endearing them to their hosts. Gradually – very gradually – things improved. The Germans helped a great deal; their bombing brought Britons and Canadians together, making the war a reality, an ordeal to be shared. The Canadians, admiring the British civilian's phlegmatic courage under bombardment, became more tolerant of his curious ways in other respects. On both sides, familiarity bred not contempt but understanding. Imperceptibly, the men from Canada were increasingly absorbed into a social system which their advanced guard in 1939 had disliked and despised.

There were many setbacks. The winter of 1941–2 was a bad moment, when miserable weather and disgust with continued idleness produced an atmosphere in which trouble sprouted freely. The German attack on Russia seemed to deprive McNaughton's men of the purpose for which they had been training – the defence of Britain against invasion. They could no longer think of the prospect of

> A six-days' stunt on an East Coast front,
> And the Hun with his back to the sea.

Some passages in a Special Report prepared by the censors on 'Relations between Canadians and British' in January 1942, reflecting the situation at the Christmas season of 1941 when there were some nasty incidents between Canadian and British soldiers (above, page 77), make unpleasant reading.[17] Witness a letter written by a woman in Reigate, Surrey: 'The damned 3rd Division has now been inflicted on us and they seem just as rough and tough as their predecessors, last night, Xmas eve they were rolling along in the middle of the road till all hours yelling at the tops of their voices, the dead drunk being dragged along by the not so drunk. If anyone wants to know what your wife thinks of Canadians just say "they stink." I heard yesterday that a local girl not quite sixteen was expecting *triplets* any moment and the Canadian responsible has bunked.' And yet a soldier of the denigrated division had written in the previous October, 'We of the 3rd Div are now getting more attention [he obviously means "favourable attention"] than when we first came over. You see the 1st and 2nd Divs really tore this little country to pieces and as a result we were all looked down upon.'[18] Probably both writers had some justification. Perhaps the 3rd Division, better disciplined than the 1st and 2nd when they first arrived, did behave rather better; and no doubt also some of its men raised Cain in Reigate at Christmas of 1941.

The other side of the relationship appears in a letter in the same 'Special Report' written by an officer of No 5 Army Field Workshop in the Ordnance Corps: 'The men have been co-operating very well as regards civilian relations and it makes things much nicer for all concerned that they have. We are at present stationed in a small town the inhabitants of which, we find, received our advent with just a bit of trepidation. Christmas went by with absolutely no riots and everybody seems to have finally decided that we aren't the kind that go around with pots of red paint and very large paint brushes. A lot of them are going to a great deal of trouble to entertain the fellows.'[19] This officer does not mention any Christmas party; but a soldier in the 5th Light Anti-Aircraft Regiment gives details of the one his unit gave for youngsters in its area:

It would do your heart good to see those dear little kids getting their gifts. They were children from the country our Padre rounded up to give a treat to and we started off by conveying them by trucks from their school-house ... and when it was over we took them back again.

There were about forty trucks and a bunch of motor cycles and weren't the kids excited. I had sixteen in with me and I sure got a big kick out of their happiness. There was a sergt. responsible for the children in each truck and they minded beautifully.[20]

Finally, a soldier of the Saskatoon Light Infantry, a 1st Division unit, writes a sentence that speaks volumes: 'We are receiving very good treatment and fine hospitality from the people in England, and most of us have a "home away from home" where we can spend our leave or visit at week-ends.'[21]

The mixed situation at Christmas of 1941, reflected in that Special Report, seems to have been the last period in the Anglo-Canadian relationship when there was any sense of crisis. A year later, in December 1942, the censors reported: 'The continuance of good relations between Canadians and British civilians is frequently referred to in the mail. It is quite evident that many of the original misunderstandings have now entirely disappeared and both sides appreciate the good qualities of each other. It is now rare to see adverse criticism.'[22]

With the passage of time the renewed prospect of action, the chance to do the job for which they had enlisted so long ago, certainly lifted the Canadians' hearts and made them more agreeable associates for the British citizenry among whom they were living. By the time when Canadian soldiers went into battle in Italy in 1943 and people were looking forward to a crossing of the Channel in 1944, victory was in the air and there was a new spirit abroad. Under these conditions, Anglo-Canadian relations were better than ever before. A censors' report on Canadian Army mail for the period 6-20 April 1944, when the Normandy D-Day was coming over the horizon, makes this memorable statement: 'The relations between British civilians and Canadian troops continue to be very cordial, and *not one adverse comment has been seen.*' (The italics are ours.) When it is considered that this report was based on the reading of 11,652 letters, its full significance becomes evident.[23]

It is fair to say that from this time relations generally remained on a very high level. In the month of the German surrender the censors commented, 'Cordial relations and a friendly spirit are being maintained between civilians and troops. Writers frequently mentioned their appreciation and gratitude for the British and England generally.' An example they quoted has its comic side; the writer was evidently a recent arrival: 'The people of London seem very nice indeed, especially to the Canadians; a personal experience of this was that I travelled a great deal on the buses and it never cost me a cent, all due to the good graces of the bus conductoresses.'[24] It is interesting that the Canadians coming to Britain in the late stages of the war exhibit little of the prickliness of the early days; they were slipping easily into a situation prepared for them by the increasingly happy experience of their predecessors.

Of course, it would be a mistake to assume that everything in the garden was invariably lovely. Even at a late stage there were unpleasant incidents. One such is described in a report of the Canadian deputy provost marshal for October 1944.[25] Fourteen Canadian soldiers from No 9 General Hospital, in Horsham, Sussex, 'were interfered with by British troops and civilians whilst proceeding to and from the hospital during the hours of darkness. The cause of the trouble is thought to be the result of jealousy or a type of "revenge" on the part of the British soldiers against the Canadians who, when stationed in that area, were friendly with their wives or sweethearts.' Other sources, including the hospital war diary, are silent about this obviously unpleasant affair. Here we have an unfortunate throwback to a situation we noted in the earliest days of the Canadian sojourn in Britain: sexual competition between

Awaiting return to Canada, a warrant officer in the Royal 22e and a paratrooper
play gin rummy at No 1 Repatriation Depot, Thursley, Surrey, in May 1945. The chevrons on the
warrant officer's sleeve indicate he had been in the service since 1939; the paratrooper wears a
wound stripe. (Arthur L. Cole, PAC / DND, PA 154976)

British and Canadian forces and hostility stemming in great part from the Canadians' higher pay. Even at this late date the relations between the forces – in Britain, not in the theatres of operations – were worse than those between the Canadians and the civil population. But in the autumn of 1944 this was definitely an isolated incident.

Who and what deserve the credit for the healthy change that had taken place? Clearly it must be widely distributed. The mere passage of time, and the better understanding that time normally brings, played a great part. The two parties to the relationship simply got to know each other better. Official effort on both sides did something. Organized recreation, organized hospitality; these played their parts. The fact that the Canadian serviceman was usually a fairly intelligent chap – that, as General McNaughton once put it in a press conference, 'our men have good common sense'[26] – certainly had a lot to do with it.

Things like this are impossible to measure. Nevertheless, looking back after forty years, many Canadians who lived through it will tell you that the chief credit is due simply to the ordinary people of Britain. Hospitality was not easy to manage there during the war; rationing was strict, there were shortages of everything; yet the British contrived to be hospitable to the strangers within their gates. In due course great numbers of Canadians found British families that in effect adopted them and gave them homes away from home. This situation certainly had a great deal to do with the thousands of marriages that took place. Personal and private hospitality meant more than the kind that was officially organized. An ex-officer recalls how much it meant to him to be told that he was welcome to come and take a bath at the vicarage when he felt disposed. This feeling gets into the letters that the censors quoted.

In the autumn of 1941 a Canadian soldier wrote, 'There isn't anything better you can do to make these lads feel good than to have them in for meals and an evening in a soft chair with pleasant company. I can tell you it's just like a breath from Heaven to go into someone's home and having the sensation of being in a place where people "live" ... I think it's one of the greatest aids there is to the war effort, because it has such a stimulating effect on the morale of the men. Please be good and kind especially to the British lads who are over there* because their folks are so good to us.'[27] In May 1945 a corporal, probably fresh from Canada, was writing, 'On my return to camp on Sunday afternoon I stopped off at Byfleet [Surrey] where I had an introduction to meet some people and stay to supper. Very interesting people and had a very pleasant time in their beautifully furnished home.'[28] The friendships formed with hospitable British families in many cases outlasted the war and some are active to this day. In fact, the war left behind it as a legacy a network of affectionate transatlantic connections whose extent is quite impossible to assess in figures but whose existence is beyond doubt.

The relationship between the Canadian serviceman and the English is utterly different from that between, say, the Canadian ex-soldier and the Dutch. The fortieth anniversary of the German surrender witnessed the return of hundreds of

*Trainees under the British Commonwealth Air Training Plan

aging Canadians to the Netherlands, a country they had liberated, and a warm welcome from the Dutch people. There were bands and applauding crowds. No such thing happened in England, and nobody would have expected it. The Canadians did not liberate Britain; they came to join in a war Britain was waging against tyranny, at a time – in the beginning – when many British people were not particularly conscious of a need for assistance. Canadian postwar pilgrimages to Britain – and there have been many of them – have been those of individuals returning quietly to a country where some of them spent years during the great conflict, and which many, almost reluctantly it sometimes seemed, came to respect and even to love. They came to renew old friendships and to revisit places they had known as youngsters in uniform – Leicester Square, Scottish communities visited on leave, airfield sites in East Anglia or Yorkshire, the Sussex Downs, a variety of little towns and villages in the south country, counties where they had 'fought' in innumerable exercises (and perhaps stolen chickens) during the years of training that preceded the grim campaigns in Italy and Northwest Europe. They saw new buildings on sites where they remembered jagged ruins, the work of German bombers. Their reunions were private and personal, not organized or distinguished by band music and parades. Subjects of the same sovereign, they may not have thought of themselves as members of the same family in the early war days, but something like family feeling had asserted itself in due course. And families do not need brass bands to express their feelings. Sometimes, too, families have family spats. Dave McIntosh remembers returning in 1953 to the airfield near Bishop's Stortford, where he served with 418 Squadron RCAF, and

trying to 'buy a drink for a local on a Sunday afternoon.' 'He turned me down flat with the comment that during the war he had had to line up outside the pub to wait for a glass, let alone a drink, because of the inside crush of drunken Canadians. I thought nine years was a bit long to bear such a grudge but, then, he was outside and I was a drunken Canadian inside.'[29] It was inevitable that the odd Briton should think interference with his own routine more important than the presence of people from abroad who had come to help his country win a desperate war. Everyone has his or her own private memories of those days, mild or bitter.

Finally, it must of course be said that the Dutch collectively are much more aware of the Canadians than the British are. Canada and the Canadians are really not as large objects on the British horizon as Britain and the British are in Canada. To Canada, Britain is one of a kind, unique; to Britain, Canada is one of a group of distant 'dominions.' The thing that distinguishes Canada is the fact that so many of her sons and daughters became temporary inhabitants of the United Kingdom during the Second World War. Even this is not particularly well remembered in Britain; but undoubtedly many British homes are well aware of it.

In 1939, when Canada and Britain went to war together against the Nazi menace, the British Empire was still in flower. Today it is a thing of the past. The Commonwealth subsists; but it is now a multi-racial affair, valuable as an instrument of conciliation when difficulties arise between its African or Asian members, helpful in international conciliation generally, but no longer the comparatively cosy family group of 1939. But for Canada, the Empire, or the Commonwealth, was always primarily a matter of the relationship with Britain; that, at least, was how the man or woman in the street saw it. 'The British connection' was the thing they were aware of. Today they are still aware of it, but somewhat less prominently than before.

The Second World War, as everyone knows, brought great changes in the world balance of power. It left two super-powers, the communist Soviet Union and the capitalist United States of America, dominating the world scene. The Pax Britannica, if it had ever really existed, was gone; the Royal Navy, which had supported it, was a decreasing shadow of its former self (though even the shadow, as the Falklands War of 1982 showed, could still be dangerous). Even the economic relationship with Britain had greatly changed. Before the war the sale of wheat to the United Kingdom had been one of the main pillars of the Canadian economy; but after the war Britain, very wisely it must be said, in effect revived the Corn Laws – agricultural protection, now largely in the form of subsidies[30] – and today produces much of the wheat required to feed herself.

Politically, then, the 'British connection' has become less important. A new Canadian prime minister nowadays makes it his first business to be – or at least to appear to be – on intimate terms with the occupant of the White House. Relations with Downing Street are on a rather lower level of significance. But a community of feeling between peoples does live on. The fact that in 1939–46 half a million Canadian service men and women spent long periods in the United Kingdom and formed warm connections there, and that some 45,000 of the men brought British wives back with them, had its due effect, which is felt to this day.

Canada and Britain have both undergone great social changes since the war. Immigration from Britain to Canada has continued on a considerable scale; but both countries have received many new citizens from lands from which few ever came before, and their outlooks on the world are bound to change somewhat as a result. Britain's joining the European Economic Community in 1973 certainly marked some shift in national orientation: henceforth the continental relationship would mean more, the old links with the overseas world less.

Today one encounters assertions that the British have no interest in Canada, that Canada is to them an unknown and invisible country where nothing ever happens.[31] This is really nothing new. At Oxford in 1927 one of the authors of this book occasionally encountered much the same attitudes. One is left indeed wondering sometimes whether the half-million we have been writing about ever really existed. Yet the incontestable fact is that they did; and their story makes some people feel that it will be strange if the affinity between Britain and Canada which has survived so many vicissitudes, and so much apparent English indifference, does not endure into the foreseeable future.

References

OST OF THE PRIMARY SOURCE MATERIAL used in the preparation of this book was found in the Public Archives of Canada, especially in Record Group (RG) 24 which is composed of records transferred to the archives by the Department of National Defence. Extensive use has been made of war diaries of units and formations and of the subject files created by Canadian Military Headquarters in London. References will also be found to subject files created at Army Headquarters, Naval Service Headquarters, and Air Force Headquarters in Ottawa as well as to the private papers of General A.G.L. McNaughton and Vice Admiral John Hughes Hallett, RN, both of which are in the PAC's Manuscript Group (MG) 30, and to the diary of the Rt Hon. Vincent Massey, which is deposited with other Massey papers at Massey College, University of Toronto.

A word of explanation is required regarding records which are described in the notes as Directorate of History (DHist) files, which are also in RG 24. When the official histories of the Canadian Army were in preparation, the staff of the Army Historical Section collected records created by the First Canadian Army, the two corps, five divisions, and by other formations for use by the historians. These records were subsequently given file and docket numbers, for example, 220C1.009 (D46). The original source of each file is indicated in the notes.

ABBREVIATIONS

AA & QMG   assistant adjutant and quartermaster general
A & Q   Administrative Branches of the Staff
AFHQ   Air Force Headquarters, Ottawa
AHQ   Army Headquarters, Ottawa
CAO   Canadian Army Overseas
CASF   Canadian Active Service Force
CMF   Central Mediterranean Force
CMHQ   Canadian Military Headquarters, London
DAG   deputy adjutant general
DA & QMG   deputy adjutant and quartermaster general
DAPC (P)   deputy assistant principal chaplain (Protestant)
DHist   Directorate of History, Department of National Defence
Div   Division
DMS   director of medical services

DPM deputy provost marshal
Fd Field
GOC-in-C general officer commanding-in-chief
MBE Member of the Order of the British Empire
MG Manuscript Group
NDHQ National Defence Headquarters
NSHQ Naval Service Headquarters
o/s Overseas
PAC Public Archives of Canada
PC Order-in-Council
RCA Royal Canadian Artillery
RCAF (WD) Royal Canadian Air Force (Women's Division)
RG Record Group
Repat Repatriation
WD War Diary

PREFACE

1 Brochure *Canada Hall* by the Rev. Canon Brian Hammond, vicar
of South Merstham. Military records of Hon. Capt. G.H.
Wolfendale, MBE. War diaries of Canadian Engineer units
concerned. Copies of various records of All Saints' Church kindly
provided by Mrs M.C. Bassett, including text of BBC broadcast,
2 May 1943
2 Cf *Report of the Ministry, Overseas Military Forces of Canada, 1918*
(London nd), 57.
3 C.P. Stacey, *Six Years of War*, Official History of the Canadian
Army in the Second World War, I (Ottawa 1955), 191
4 C.P. Stacey, *Arms, Men and Governments: The War Policies of Canada,*

1939–1945 (Ottawa 1970), 305. Information from Directorate of
History, National Defence Headquarters, Ottawa

CHAPTER 1: THE MILITARY TASK

1 C.P. Stacey, *The Canadian Army, 1939–1945* (Ottawa 1948), 5
2 Stacey, *Six Years of War*, I, 50
3 Ibid., 258–63
4 Ibid., 265–9. Massey Diary, 24 May 1940
5 Stacey, *Six Years of War*, 269–95. C.P. Stacey, *Arms, Men and
Governments*, 32–3
6 Stacey, *Six Years of War*, 87–99
7 Ibid., 244
8 Stacey, *Arms, Men and Governments*, 230–1
9 Ibid., 233–5, and *Six Years of War*, 249–51
10 Stacey, *Six Years of War*, 308
11 Ibid., chaps. X-XII. One good book is Ronald Atkin, *Dieppe 1942:
The Jubilee Disaster* (London 1980).
12 G.W.L. Nicholson, *The Canadians in Italy, 1943–1945*, Official
History of the Canadian Army in the Second World War, II
(Ottawa 1956), chaps. I and II
13 Stacey, *Arms, Men and Governments*, 231–47
14 Nicholson, *The Canadians in Italy*, 681
15 J.W. Pickersgill, *The Mackenzie King Record*, I (Ottawa 1960), 607
16 This account is summarized from C.P. Stacey, *The Victory
Campaign*, Official History of the Canadian Army in the Second
World War, III (Ottawa 1960).
17 F.J. Hatch, *Aerodrome of Democracy: Canada and the British
Commonwealth Air Training Plan, 1939–1945* (Ottawa 1983), 206

18 Stacey, *Arms, Men and Governments*, 28

19 D.J. Goodspeed, ed., *The Armed Forces of Canada, 1867–1967* (Ottawa 1967), 166. Since at the time of writing the official history of the RCAF has not yet covered the whole period of the Second World War, this is probably the best summary at present available.

20 Map of Bomber Command stations in Sir Charles Webster and Noble Frankland, *The Strategic Air Offensive Against Germany 1939–1945*, 4 vols. (London 1961), III, opposite 126

21 Ibid., 287. The fascinating memoirs of a Canadian pilot serving in an RAF bomber squadron is Murray Peden, *A Thousand Shall Fall* (Stittsville, Ont. 1979). The story of a pilot in a Canadian squadron is J. Douglas Harvey, *Boys, Bombs and Brussels Sprouts* (Toronto 1981). Another RCAF narrative is Dave McIntosh, *Terror in the Starboard Seat* (Toronto 1980).

22 Webster and Frankland, *Strategic Air Offensive*, IV, app. 41. Ground staff are not included.

23 C.P. Stacey, *Canada and the Age of Conflict*, II: *1921–48: The Mackenzie King Era* (Toronto 1981), 276n

24 The story of the Royal Canadian Navy is told in two not entirely satisfactory official publications, Gilbert Norman Tucker, *The Naval Service of Canada: Its Official History*, 2 vols. (Ottawa 1952), and Joseph Schull, *The Far Distant Ships* (Ottawa 1950). Two valuable recent unofficial books are Marc Milner, *North Atlantic Run: The Royal Canadian Navy and the Battle for the Convoys* (Toronto 1985), and Michael L. Hadley, *U-Boats Against Canada: German Submarines in Canadian Waters* (Kingston and Montreal 1985). See also the essays in James A. Boutilier, ed., *The RCN in Retrospect, 1910–1968* (Vancouver 1982).

25 See the informative map between pages 201 and 204 in Goodspeed, ed., *The Armed Forces of Canada.*

26 Stacey, *Arms, Men and Governments*, 323

27 Tucker, *Naval Service of Canada*, II, chap. 16

CHAPTER 2: GETTING ACQUAINTED

1 War diary, Royal Regiment of Canada, September 1939, Public Archives of Canada, Record Group 24, vol. 15,224

2 Stacey, *Six Years of War*, app. B

3 *Canada Year Book*, 1940, 751

4 App. B-1 to report by Professor E.A. Bott, CMHQ file 42/BOTT/1, RG 24, vol. 12,775. WD, director of medical services CMHQ, 16 June 1941, RG 24, vol. 15,645

5 'Semi-Annual Report of the Activities of the Dominion Troops Information Bureau' copy in WD, staff capt. auxiliary services, HQ Cdn Base Units, Bordon, April 1941, RG 24, vol. 16,664. WD, asst director auxiliary services, Jan. 1940, RG 24, vol. 16,664

6 C.P. Stacey, *The Arts of War and Peace*, Historical Documents of Canada, V (Toronto 1972), 180–9. Cf the sketch by Donald Creighton, 'Wines, Spirits, and Provincial Politicians,' in *The Passionate Observer* (Toronto 1980), 65–70.

7 Stacey, *Six Years of War*, 232, 419

8 Ibid., 419

9 Seaforth Highlanders of Canada, 30 May 1940, RG 24, vol. 15,253

10 Farley Mowat, *The Regiment* (Toronto 1955), 27

11 Undated copy enclosed in Pearson to Crerar, 2 July 1940, CMHQ file 20/1 DIV/1, RG 24, vol. 12,714

12 WD, A & Q Branch, Rear HQ 1st Cdn Div, July 1940, app. 14, RG 24, vol. 13,734
13 31 May 1940, RG 24, vol. 15,206
14 Webster and Frankland, *Strategic Air Offensive*, III, 287
15 Stacey, *Six Years of War*, 197
16 WD, A & Q Branch, HQ Cdn Corps [7th Corps], 9 Nov. 1940, RG 24, vol. 13,692
17 WD, 1st Cdn Pioneer Battalion, Oct. 1940, app. 7, RG 24, vol. 14,815. *The Canadians in Britain, 1939–1944*, The Canadian Army at War, No 1, 2nd ed. (Ottawa 1946), 98
18 *The Canadians in Britain*, 92–7
19 The grim monthly statistics are collected in Royal Institute of International Affairs, *Chronology of the Second World War* (London and New York 1947). On the early Blitz, a still excellent account is the contemporary British official booklet, *Front Line, 1940–41* (London 1942).
20 *Chronology of the Second World War*, 162–339
21 Ibid., 344. Stacey, *Six Years of War*, 299n. Hans Rumpf, *The Bombing of Germany* (London 1963), 164
22 Typescript history of the Corps of Canadian Fire Fighters, Department of Veterans Affairs, RG 38, vol. 141. For an account of its organization see DVA file 49-10-4, RG 38, vol. 140.
23 CMHQ file 20/GEN/1, RG 24, vol. 12,715
24 WD, A & Q Branch, HQ 7th Corps, Oct. 1940, RG 24, vol. 13,692
25 Documents on CMHQ file 20/GEN/1, see note 23, above.
26 WD, 2nd Fd Regt RCA, Dec. 1940 and Feb. 1941, RG 24, vol. 14,415
27 WD, 1st Cdn Divisional Signals, Sept. and Dec. 1940, RG 24, vol. 14,927
28 See *Canada's Weekly* (London), 3 Jan. 1941.

29 Stacey, *Six Years of War*, 207–10
30 N.H. Carrier and J.R. Jeffery, *External Migration: A Study of the Available Statistics, 1815–1950*, Studies on Medical and Population Subjects (London 1953), table III
31 *Canada Year Book*, 1938, 143
32 Field Censors (Home) report, 4–18 July 1942, CMHQ file 4/CENSOR/4/7, RG 24, vol. 12,319
33 See, for example, WD, 7th Light Anti-Aircraft Regt RCA, 22 Jan. 1942, RG 24, vol. 14,605.
34 DHist file 221C1 (D270), RG 24, vol. 10,771
35 DHist file 181.009 (D283), formerly a file of RCAF Headquarters Overseas, file retained by DHist
36 Stacey, *Arms, Men and Governments*, app. D
37 DHist file 181.009 (D283), note 35, above.
38 Ibid., Report No C10, letter dated 6 June 1941
39 Ibid., letter dated 8 June 1942 [1941?]
40 Information from Colin Friesen, bursar of Massey College, formerly pilot officer, 150 Squadron RAF. Letter Peden to Stacey, 31 Oct. 1986
41 DHist file 181.009 (D283), note 35, above, letter dated 13 June 1941
42 Ibid., letter dated 31 May 1941
43 Ibid., letters dated 10 June 1941
44 Ibid., Report No C7, letter dated 4 April 1941
45 Ibid., Report No C10, letter dated 31 May 1941
46 Ibid., Report No C10
47 Ibid., Supplement to Report No C13
48 Ibid.
49 Ibid., undated letter, Report No C10
50 Peden, *A Thousand Shall Fall*, 170, 231

51 DHist file 181.009 (D283), note 35, above, letter dated 5 June 1941
52 NSHQ file NSC 4050-7, RG 24, accession 83–84/167, box 1342
53 Robert Collins, *The Long and the Short and the Tall* (Saskatoon 1986), 87–9; Donald A. Fraser, *Live to Look Again* (Belleville, Ont. 1984), 52, 60; Harvey, *Boys, Bombs and Brussels Sprouts*, 78–80; Peden, *A Thousand Shall Fall*, 118

CHAPTER 3: COMRADES IN ARMS

1 CMHQ file 4/CENSOR/4/1, RG 24, vol. 12,318
2 'Morale ... 1 Cdn Div,' 9 Jan. 1942, DHist file 220C1.009 (D47), formerly a file of HQ 1st Cdn Corps, RG 24, vol. 10,752
3 Thompson to McNaughton, 29 April 1940, DHist file 230C1 (D135), formerly a file of HQ 1st Cdn Div, RG 24, vol. 10,849
4 DHist file 230C1 (D135)
5 CMHQ file 20/REPORTS/2, RG 24, vol. 12,723
6 CMHQ file 20/REPORTS/3, ibid.
7 Field Censors (Home) report, 5–19 Jan. 1942, CMHQ file 4/CENSOR/4/4, RG 24, vol. 12,318
8 Field Censors (Home) Special Report, Jan. 1941, CMHQ file 4/CENSOR/4/4, ibid. See also WD, AA & QMG, Cdn Reinforcement Units, Dec. 1941, app. 70, RG 24, vol. 16,687; WD, No 1 Cdn Armoured Corps Reinforcement Unit, Dec. 1941, RG 24, vol. 16,718.
9 CMHQ file 20/REPORTS/13, July 1943 and Oct. 1944, RG 24, vol. 12,723
10 Field Censors (Home) report, 21 July–5 Aug. 1943, CMHQ file 4/CENSOR REPS/ 1/2, RG 24, vol. 12,321. For some personal reminiscences of contacts with British service people see William C. Heine, *Kooks and Dukes, Counts and No-Accounts* (Edmonton 1986), 161–2, 170–1.
11 Ibid. See also Kathleen Robson Roe, *War Letters from the C.W.A.C.* (Toronto 1975), 68.
12 *The Canadians in Britain, 1939–1944*, 2nd ed. (Ottawa 1946), 165
13 Clipping in WD, A & Q Branch, HQ 1st Cdn Corps, Aug. 1942, RG 24, vol. 13,694
14 *Canada's Weekly* (London), 1 Oct. 1943
15 Censorship report, CMF [Central Mediterranean Force] series, No 40, 1–15 March 1944, CMHQ file 4/CENSOR REPS/3, RG 24, vol. 12,323
16 Norman Longmate, *The GIs: The Americans in Britain, 1942–1945* (London 1975). Leslie Thomas, *The Magic Army* (London 1981)
17 David Reynolds, 'The Churchill Government and the Black American Troops in Britain during World War II,' *Transactions of the Royal Historical Society*, 5th Series, 35 (1985): 132
18 Field Censors (Home) report, 24 Aug.–3 Sept. 1942, CMHQ file 4/CENSOR/4/8, RG 24, vol. 12,314
19 David Reynolds, 'GI and Tommy in Wartime Britain: The Army "Inter-Attachment" Scheme of 1943–44,' *Journal of Strategic Studies* (Dec. 1984): 415
20 Personal recollection. E.R. Chamberlin, *Life in Wartime Britain* (London 1972), 157
21 'The First Canadian Army,' *Fortune*, Jan. 1944
22 Field Censors (Home) report, 6–20 July 1943, CMHQ file 4/CENSOR REPS/1/2, RG 24, vol. 12,321
23 Censorship report, Canadian units in 21 Army Group, 1 June 1944, in Stacey, *Six Years of War*, 424
24 Field Censors (Home) reports, 21 July–5 Aug. 1943 and 6–21 Nov. 1943, CMHQ files 4/CENSOR REPS/1/2 and 1/3, RG 24, vol. 12,321

25 Reports of DPM Cdn Provost Corps Overseas in CMHQ file 20/REPORTS/13, RG 24, vol. 12,723

26 Reynolds, 'GI and Tommy'

27 *The Times*, London, 5 June 1944. The complainant was Dennis Kendall, MP for Grantham.

28 Field Censors (Home) report, 6–21 Nov. 1943, CMHQ file 4/CENSOR REPS/1/3, RG 24, vol. 12,321

29 Brig.-Gen. Whitaker's file on the game, kindly lent to the authors; documents (including text of Leather broadcast) in CMHQ file 23/SPORTS/18, RG 24, vol. 10,171

30 Gordon A. Harrison, *Cross Channel Attack*, United States Army in World War II (Washington 1951), 158n, 327

31 Toronto *Evening Telegram*, 21 March 1944. For the basic arrangements for the game see memo by Brig. E.G. Weeks, 23 Feb. 1944, on CMHQ file 23/SPORTS/18 and other papers on the same file.

32 Diary, Historical Officer, CMHQ, 19 March 1944, being kept at this time by Major G.F.G. Stanley, RG 24, vol. 13,408

33 Field Censors (Home) report, 6–20 Sept. 1943, CMHQ file 4/CENSOR REPS/1/2, RG 24, vol. 12,321

34 Censorship report, CMF series, No 40, 1–15 March 1944, note 15, above

CHAPTER 4: KEEPING THE TROOPS HAPPY

1 Massey Diary, 22 Aug. 1940

2 On Protestant chaplains see Hon. Major Walter T. Steven, *In This Sign* (Toronto 1948). For a Protestant chaplain's story see Waldo E.L. Smith, *What Time the Tempest* (Toronto 1953); for a Roman Catholic's, R.M. Hickey, *The Scarlet Dawn* (Campbellton, NB 1949).

3 Stacey, *Six Years of War*, 421

4 Ibid., 421–2

5 Alan M. Hurst, *The Canadian Y.M.C.A. in World War II* (np, nd), 161

6 Canadian YMCA Overseas, Report of Operations Month of March 1943, CMHQ file 26/YMCA/1, RG 24, vol. 10,185

7 Stacey, *Six Years of War*, 422

8 Field Censors (Home) report, 10–23 Nov. 1941, CMHQ file 4/CENSOR/1/1, RG 24, vol. 12,318

9 Capt. Victor MacLean, Auxiliary Services, 1 Cdn Div, to CMHQ, 20 April 1940, CMHQ file 23/SPORTS/1, RG 24, vol. 10,168

10 WD, Hastings and Prince Edward Regiment, Jan. and March 1940, RG 24, vol. 15,070

11 RCAF HQ to senior officer of auxiliary services, CMHQ, 25 Oct. 1940, CMHQ file 23/RCAF/1, RG 24, vol. 10,163

12 Documents in CMHQ file 23/SPORTS/1, RG 24, vol. 10,168

13 Report in CMHQ file 26/YMCA/1, RG 24, vol. 10,185

14 Report in CMHQ file 23/SPORTS/1, note 12, above

15 Naval Service Headquarters file NS 800-10-2/1, RG 24, vols. 3480–1

16 CMHQ file 26/YMCA/1, note 13, above

17 CMHQ file 23/LIBRARIES/1, RG 24, vol. 10,157

18 On prostitution in wartime Britain see Edward Smithies, *Crime in Wartime: A Social History of Crime in World War II* (London 1982), chap. 8.

19 WD, asst director of auxiliary services overseas, March 1940, RG 24, vol. 16,664. Meeting, 2 Oct. 1940, CMHQ file23/MISC/1, RG 24,

vol. 10.157. Information from Brig.-Gen. W.D. Whitaker

20 Information from Patricia Macoun

21 British Columbia Monthly News Letter, Jan. 1940, CMHQ file 26/B.C. HOUSE/1, RG 24, vol. 10,179

22 Massey Diary, passim. 'The Beaver Club: Canada's New Headquarters in London,' press release, 23 Feb. 1940, CMHQ file 26/BEAVER/1, RG 24, vol. 10,179

23 Ibid.

24 Field Censors (Home) report, 1–14 May 1945, CMHQ file 4/CENSOR REPS/1/7, RG 24, vol. 12,322

25 Massey Diary, 20 July, 24 Aug., and 26 Sept. 1942

26 Ibid., 4 May 1942. Report by Col. Hon. R.J. Manion on Auxiliary Services Overseas, 1941, CMHQ file 23/VISITS/2, RG 24, vol. 10,173

27 Personal recollection, and many references in Massey Diary

28 WD, senior chaplain (RC), HQ First Cdn Army, 14 Feb. 1944, RG 24, vol. 15,631

29 What's Past Is Prologue: The Memoirs of the Right Honourable Vincent Massey (Toronto 1963)

30 Various references in Stacey, Arms, Men and Governments, and Canada and the Age of Conflict, II

31 Massey Diary, 27 May 1940. Cf Scott Young, Red Shield in Action: A Record of Canadian Salvation Army War Services in the Second Great War (np 1949), 48.

32 Massey Diary, 25 Dec. 1942

33 Stacey, Six Years of War, 296n

34 Memo for Office of High Commissioner from asst director auxiliary services, 3 Oct. 1944, CMHQ file 23/WELFARE/1, RG 24, vol. 10,174. Hurst, Canadian Y.M.C.A. in World War II, 186–9

35 Memo, 3 Oct. 1944, note 34, above; Hurst, Canadian Y.M.C.A. in World War II, 286–9

36 Memo, 3 Oct. 1944, note 34, above

37 Young, Red Shield in Action, 69

38 Field Censors (Home) report, 6–20 Feb. 1944, CMHQ file 4/CENSOR REPS/1/5, RG 24, vol. 12,322

39 Ibid., 4–19 Nov. 1942, 4/CENSOR/4/9, RG 24, vol. 12,319

40 Meeting 14 May 1941, CMHQ file 23/MISC/1, RG 24, vol. 10,157

41 Raymond Massey, A Hundred Different Lives (Toronto 1979), 288–94

42 WD, asst director auxiliary services, 12 Dec. 1941, RG 24, vol. 16,664

43 Ibid., 15 Sept., 9 Oct. 1941

44 Massey Diary, 9 Oct. 1941

45 Field Censors (Home) report, 10–23 Nov. 1941, CMHQ file 4/CENSOR/4/4, RG 24, vol. 12,318

46 WD, asst director auxiliary services, 16 Dec. 1941, RG 24, vol. 16,664

47 Ibid., 28 July 1944, RG 24, vol. 16,665

48 Air Force Headquarters files 250-14-1, RG 24, vol. 3288; 250-14-2, RG 24, vol. 3289; and 250-14-14, RG 24, vol. 3291

49 On arrival overseas see WD, asst director auxiliary services, 22 Dec. 1943, RG 24, vol. 13,479. Field Censors (Home) report, 21 Feb.–5 March 1944, CMHQ file 4/CENSOR REPS/1/5, RG 24, vol. 12,322. Letters from W. Victor George in Globe and Mail, Toronto, 4 and 11 Jan. 1983

50 Massey Diary, 1 Feb. 1945

51 Field Censors (Home) report, 1–15 May 1945, CMHQ file 4/CENSOR REPS/1/7, RG 24, vol. 12,322. Personal recollection

52 Documents on CMHQ file 4/PRESS/20, RG 24, vol. 12,372

53 On the *Maple Leaf* see Richard S. Malone, *A Portrait of War* (Toronto 1983), 221ff, and *A World in Flames* (Toronto 1984), 82ff. 'Bing' Coughlin and J.D. MacFarlane, *Herbie!* (np, nd).

54 Documents on CMHQ file 4/PRESS/20, note 52, above. Illustration and caption opposite page 483 in Stacey, *Six Years of War*

55 Air Force Headquarters file 300-3-6, RG 24, vol. 3333. Cf. 'Wild about Journalism,' *Alumni Gazette*, University of Western Ontario, spring 1983.

56 CMHQ file 4/BROADCAST/22, RG 24, vol. 12,314; see also CMHQ file 4/BROADCAST/10, RG 24, vol. 12,311.

57 Field Censors (Home) report, 13–26 Oct. 1941, CMHQ file 4/CENSOR/4/3, RG 24, vol. 12,318

58 Canadian Postal Corps file 'Services to Canadian Armed Forces During World War II,' RG 24, vol. 6652

59 Reference in Stacey personal letter

60 WD, asst director of Army Postal Services, CMHQ, 5 Sept. 1941, RG 24, vol. 16,360

61 Air Force Headquarters file 935/2–1, RG 24, vol. 17,982

62 Letter from Mr Peden to Stacey, 9 Nov. 1985

63 Memo by Brig. P.J. Montague, 22 July 1940, PAC, McNaughton Papers, MG 30, E 133, vol. 188, file 5-8-1, vol. 1

64 McNaughton file, note 63, above

65 Douglas LePan, *Bright Glass of Memory* (Toronto 1979)

66 Ibid. Memo by J.B. Bickersteth, 21 Dec. 1940, McNaughton file, note 63, above

67 LePan, *Bright Glass of Memory*, 19–22. Memo, LePan to GOC -in-c, First Cdn Army, on the British Council, 15 July 1943, CMHQ file 61/BCA/1, RG 24, vol. 10,274

68 Field Censors (Home) report, 21 Feb.–5 March 1944, CMHQ file 4/CENSOR REPS/1/5, RG 24, vol. 12,322

69 Letter by Stacey, 26 July 1942

70 LePan to GOC-in-C, First Cdn Army, 26 Jan. 1943, McNaughton Papers, file 5-8-1, vol. 3

71 Canadian Army Overseas Routine Orders 5970, 5972, and 6038 (1945). A personal account by Brig. Beament, 'The Khaki University of Canada in the United Kingdom, 1945–46,' was published in *As You Were*, a publication of the Royal Military College Club of Canada, in 1984.

72 Diary, Historical Officer, CMHQ, 20 Sept. 1945, RG 24, vol. 13,408

73 Progress Report No 10 of Khaki University, CMHQ file 61/KHAKI UNIVERSITY/1/4, RG 24, vol. 10,282

CHAPTER 5: LONELY CANADIANS, BRITISH WOMEN

1 Massey Diary, 21 June 1942

2 PC 2371 of 4 June 1940

3 5 July 1943. DHist file 219C1.009 (D52), formerly a file of A & Q Branch, HQ First Cdn Army, RG 24, vol. 10,725

4 WD, senior chaplain (RC), HQ, Canadian Reinforcement Units, Nov. 1943, RG 24, vol. 15,629

5 CMHQ file 20/1 DIV/1, RG 24, vol. 12,714

6 DAG, CMHQ to W.H. Dudley, 14 Aug. 1940, CMHQ file 6/MARRY/1/1, RG 24, vol. 12,497

7 Air Force Headquarters file 828-15, vol. 3, RG 24, vol. 17,803

8 CASF (O/S) Routine Orders 520 and 576

9 WD, DA & QMG, Cdn Corps, July 1941, RG 24, vol. 13,692, Remarks by Maj.-Gen. G.R. Pearkes

10 Memo to DAG, CMHQ, 24 April 1941, CMHQ file 6/MARRY/1/1,

note 6, above

11 CAO Routine Order 1262

12 Instructions, undated, CMHQ file 6/MARRY/1/1, note 6, above

13 WD, Chaplain Service (P), CMHQ, June-July 1941, RG 24, vol. 15,632

14 WD, senior chaplain (RC), 3rd Cdn Div, Nov. 1943, RG 24, vol. 15,629

15 WD, senior chaplain (RC), First Cdn Army, July 1943, ibid.

16 CMHQ file 6/MARRY/1/1, note 6, above

17 WD, Chaplain Service (RC), CMHQ, Jan. 1943, RG 24, vol. 15,629

18 Returns on CMHQ file 6/BIRTHS/1, RG 24, vol. 12,444

19 Ibid.

20 Ibid. NDHQ Army file HQ 650-124-33, RG 24, vol. 6545

21 See, for example, John Patrick Grogan, *Dieppe and Beyond for a Dollar and a Half a Day* (Renfrew, Ont. 1982), 117.

22 File HQ 650-124-33, note 20, above

23 WD, senior chaplain (P), 1st Cdn Div, Sept. 1941, RG 24, vol. 15,632; WD, senior chaplain (RC), 2nd Cdn Div, July 1943, RG 24, vol. 15,629

24 'Marriages of Canadian Servicemen in the UK and Notes on the Canadian Government's Arrangements for Passages to Canada of their Wives and Children,' CMHQ file 65/PRESS/1, RG 24, vol. 10,333

25 CMHQ file 65/ADMIN CWB/1, RG 24, vol. 10,324. History of the Directorate of Repatriation, NDHQ Army file HQ 650-124-33, note 20, above

26 Carrier and Jeffery, *External Migration: A Study of the Available Statistics, 1815–1950*, 39

27 Michael Crabb, 'Tributes for a Wellspring of Ballet,' *Maclean's*, 3 Dec. 1984

28 Stacey, *Six Years of War,* 210

29 WD, RCAF (WD) Overseas, PAC microfilm reel C-12,412. This diary deals with all WD activities in Britain.

30 G.N. Tucker, *The Naval Service of Canada: Its Official History,* 2 vols. (Ottawa 1952), II, 322

31 W.R. Feasby, ed., *Official History of the Canadian Medical Services, 1939–1945,* 2 vols. (Ottawa 1953–6), I, 312, 331, 329, 361; Stacey, *Six Years of War,* 206

32 Jean Bruce, *Back the Attack! Canadian Women during the Second World War—at Home and Abroad* (Toronto 1985), chap. 9

33 NDHQ Army file HQ 54-27-1-21, vol. 2, RG 24, vol. 2050

34 Col. C.H. Walker to Andrew Bell, 2 Aug. 1945, ibid.

35 Jean M. Ellis, with Isabel Dingman, *Face Powder and Gunpowder* (Toronto 1947), 37–9

36 Chambers to Lt-Col. R.F. Sheppard, 12 March 1946, CMHQ file 23/DOM REL/1/3, RG 24, vol. 10,145. Massey Diary, 28 Jan. 1946. On Black fund see CMHQ file 26/W.A.B. FUND/1, RG 24, vol. 10,185.

37 WD, director of medical services, CMHQ, 2 and 5 Dec. 1939, 12 April 1940, RG 24, vol. 15,645

38 Ibid., 19 May 1941

39 Ibid., 24 Oct. 1941

40 WD, No 1 Cdn Special Hospital, Oct. 1941, RG 24, vol. 15,714

41 WD, DMS, CMHQ, 25 Aug. 1941, note 37, above

42 Ibid., 17 Dec. 1941

43 Annual Report on the Health of the Canadian Army Overseas for 1942, App. 1 to WD, DMS, CMHQ, May 1943, note 37, above

44 WD, DMS, CMHQ, Dec. 1942, note 37, above

45 Minutes of meeting, CMHQ file 11/HYGIENE/1, RG 24, vol. 12,612. WD, DMS, CMHQ, June 1943, note 37, above

46 DHist file 133.063 (D18F), RG 24, vol. 18,576
47 CMHQ file 11/HYGIENE VD/5, RG 24, vol 12,612
48 CAO Routine Order 4752
49 CMHQ file 11/HYGIENE VD/8, RG 24, vol. 12,613
50 Ibid.
51 WD, DMS, CMHQ, March 1945, App. 3, note 37, above
52 Ibid., June 1945, App. 2
53 Ibid., Aug. 1945, App. 2
54 Ibid., Oct. 1945, App. 4. Feasby, ed., *Canadian Medical Services*, II, 443
55 Feasby, *Canadian Medical Services*, II, 512–15
56 Public Record Office file Air 2/5995. William Carter has most kindly lent us his photocopy of this file.
57 Ibid.
58 Ibid.
59 Ibid.
60 Ibid.
61 Ibid., 16 Sept. 1943
62 Ibid.
63 Ibid., Brown to Sinclair, 21 Aug. 1941; Sinclair to Brown, 11 Sept. 1941
64 Feasby, *Canadian Medical Services*, II, 513
65 Surgeon Lt-Cmdr H.G. Baker to Canadian Naval Mission Overseas, 17 and 26 Nov., 8 Dec. 1945; to medical director general, RCN, 19 Jan. 1945, Naval Service Headquarters file NS 4478-1, vol. 3, PAC Accession 83-84/167, box 1592
66 Report of senior chaplain (P), 1st Cdn Div, Jan. 1943, DHist file 229C1.99 (D33), formerly a file of DAPC (P), 1st Cdn Corps, RG 24, vol. 10,834

67 Stacey, *Six Years of War*, 428
68 Copy in CMHQ file 19/CANADA/2, RG 24, vol. 10,103
69 Stacey, *Six Years of War*, 429
70 For detail see ibid., 430–1.
71 Air Force Headquarters file 247-1-2, RG 24, vol. 10,105
72 *The Canadian Summer: The Memoirs of James Alan Roberts* (Toronto 1981), 153–9, 168–9, 173–4

CHAPTER 6: THE SEAMY SIDE

1 Stacey, *Six Years of War*, 255–6
2 *The Times*, London, 5 Aug. 1942
3 Stacey, *Six Years of War*, 426n
4 Smithies, *Crime in Wartime*, 157
5 Documents on CMHQ file 20/CIVIL/1, RG 24, vol. 12,708. Massey Diary, 19 Nov. 1940
6 DHist file 221C1 (D270), formerly a file of GOC, 1st Cdn Corps, RG 24, vol. 10,771
7 CMHQ file 12/PAY/1, RG 24, vol. 10,036
8 Massey Diary, 3 April 1941
9 Memo, 22 Dec. 1940. WD, A & Q Branch, HQ 7th Corps, Dec. 1940, RG 24, vol. 13,692
10 On the Witley riots of 1919 see Desmond Morton, *A Peculiar Kind of Politics* (Toronto 1982), 195–7.
11 Documents on CMHQ file 12/PAY/1, note 7, above
12 21 June 1941
13 CMHQ file 20/OFFENCE/1. The report appears as Appendix A in Report No 119, Historical Officer CMHQ, 30 June 1944 (DHist records).

14 Ibid.

15 Ibid.

16 See the discussion in Stacey, *Six Years of War*, 425–7.

17 Canadian Press dispatch in *Globe and Mail*, Toronto, 17 Jan. 1942

18 *News of the World*, London, 25 Jan. 1942

19 Documents in DHist file 219C1.009 (D52), formerly a file of A & Q Branch, First Cdn Army, RG 24, vol. 10,725. Pownall's own letter is not present.

20 Ibid., draft letter 18 Sept. 1943 and minute by McNaughton

21 *Brighton and Hove Herald*, 17 July 1943; *West Sussex Gazette*, 15 July 1943; *Times*, 27 July, 27 Aug. 1943

22 Noël Coward, *Future Indefinite* (London 1954), 234–5

23 Montgomery to Crerar, 28 June 1942; Crerar to Montgomery, 3 July 1942, DHist file 221C1 (D270), formerly a file of GOC, 1st Cdn Corps, RG 24, vol. 10,771

24 9 July 1942, ibid

25 Field Censors (Home) report, 29 Sept.–12 Oct. 1941, CMHQ file 4/CENSOR/4/3, RG 24, vol. 12,318

26 Massey Diary, 6 Dec. 1941

27 PAC, unpublished Hughes Hallett memoirs, MG 30, E 463, 163; Stacey, *Six Years of War*, 337

28 J. Douglas Harvey, *Boys, Bombs and Brussels Sprouts*, paperback edition (Toronto 1983), 83

29 Extract from report of public relations officer, CMHQ, week ending 14 Nov. 1942, McNaughton Papers, vol. 150, file 3-7-13

30 British statute 20 Geo. 5, c. 22, part II; royal assent, 29 April 1930

31 War Office to senior officer, CMHQ, 31 July 1940, CMHQ file 20/DET BKS/1, RG 24, vol. 12,714

32 Cable CMHQ to NDHQ, 8 March 1941, ibid.

33 Memo by Lt-Col. A.D. Cameron, 29 May 1942, ibid.

34 Wing Commander J.A.R. Mason to senior officer, CMHQ, 23 March 1943, ibid.

35 Ibid.

36 WD, No 4 Cdn Military Prison and Detention Barracks (Reading), 10 May 1945, RG 24, vol. 16,521

37 Clipping in CMHQ file 4/PRESS/11, RG 24, vol. 12,370

38 WD, No 4 Cdn Military and Detention Barracks, May 1945, text and App. 2, and No 5 Cdn Military Prison and Detention Barracks (Alton), July–Nov. 1945, note 36, above

CHAPTER 7: SIX YEARS OF IT

1 Pamphlet *After Victory in Europe*, issued by CMHQ, May 1945

2 Stacey, *Six Years of War*, 432

3 Ibid., 432

4 Col. G.W.L. Nicholson, *Canadian Expeditionary Force, 1914–1919*, Official History of the Canadian Army in the First World War (Ottawa 1962), 532

5 Ibid. More detail may be found in Morton, *A Peculiar Kind of Politics*, 186–98. See also Morton's '"Kicking and Complaining": Demobilization Riots in the Canadian Expeditionary Force, 1918–19,' *Canadian Historical Review*, Sept. 1980.

6 Stacey, *Six Years of War*, 433. On courts martial see CMHQ file 20/ALDERSHOT/2, RG 24, vol. 12,705.

7 Report on letters examined 16–31 July 1945, 21 Army Group, CMHQ file 4/CENSOR REPS/2/4, RG 24, vol. 12,322

8 Stacey, *Six Years of War*, 424

9 WD, 1 Cdn Repat Depot, 29 Jan. 1946, RG 24, vol. 16,814

10 CMHQ file 20/COMMEND/1, RG 24, vol. 12,710
11 Ibid.
12 Undated letter, ibid.
13 Nicholson, *Canadian Expeditionary Force*, 532. C.P. Stacey, *The Canadian Army, 1939–1945*, 309
14 *After Victory in Europe*, 11
15 CMHQ file 8/DIS/11, RG 24, vol. 9349
16 History of the Directorate of Repatriation, NDHQ file HQ 650-124-33, RG 24, vol. 6545
17 Special Report, Jan. 1942, CMHQ file 4/CENSOR/4/4, RG 24, vol. 12,318
18 CMHQ file 4/CENSOR/4/3, RG 24, vol. 12,318
19 Special Report, note 17, above
20 Ibid.
21 Ibid.

22 CMHQ file 4/CENSOR/4/9, RG 24, vol. 12,319
23 Stacey, *Six Years of War*, 424
24 Field Censors (Home) report, 1–15 May 1945, CMHQ file 4/CENSOR REPS/1/7, RG 24, vol. 12,723
25 Report for Oct. 1944, DPM Canadian Provost Corps Overseas, CMHQ file 20/REPORTS/13, RG 24, vol. 12,723
26 Stacey, *Six Years of War*, 427
27 Field Censors (Home) report, 27 Oct.–9 Nov. 1941, CMHQ file 4/CENSOR REPS/4/3, RG 24, vol. 12,318
28 Field Censors (Home) report, 1–15 May 1945, note 24, above
29 Letter to Stacey, 23 May 1985
30 *Annual Register*, 1947, 501; 1948, 460
31 For example, Sandra Gwyn, 'Over Home,' *Saturday Night* Anniversary Issue, 1987

Index